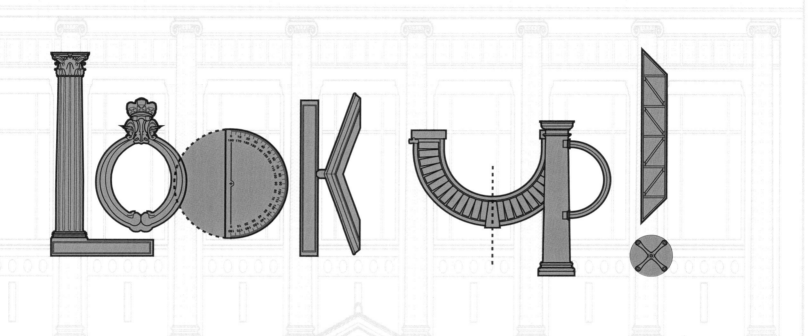

by Lauren Rubin

Inspired by Aubrey & Ian

Publishers of Architecture, Art, and Design
Gordon Goff: Publisher

www.oroeditions.com
info@oroeditions.com

Published by ORO Editions

Graphic Design: Lauren Rubin and Laura Knight Keating
Text: Laura Knight Keating
Illustrations: The team at Lauren Rubin Architecture with Audrey Choi, Katrazyna Kuta, and Rebecca Kent
Color Renderings: Amelia Modlin
Project Coordinator: Kirby Anderson

10 9 8 7 6 5 4 3 2 First Edition

Library of Congress data available upon request. World Rights: Available

ISBN: 978-1-943532-17-9

Color Separations and Printing: ORO Group Ltd.
Printed in China.

International Distribution: www.oroeditions.com/distribution

ORO Editions makes a continuous effort to minimize the overall carbon footprint of its publications. As part of this goal, ORO Editions, in association with Global ReLeaf, arranges to plant trees to replace those used in the manufacturing of the paper produced for its books. Global ReLeaf is an international campaign run by American Forests, one of the world's oldest nonprofit conservation organizations. Global ReLeaf is American Forests' education and action program that helps individuals, organizations, agencies, and corporations improve the local and global environment by planting and caring for trees.

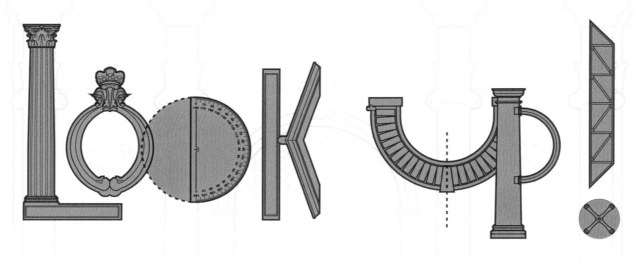

NEW YORK CITY

HOW TO USE THIS BOOK

LOOK UP! + LEARN! | DESIGN! + DRAW!

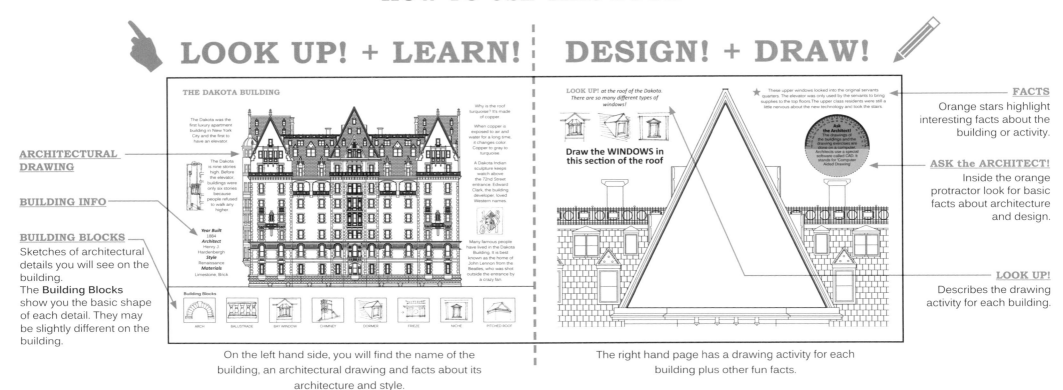

ARCHITECTURAL DRAWING

BUILDING INFO

BUILDING BLOCKS
Sketches of architectural details you will see on the building.
The **Building Blocks** show you the basic shape of each detail. They may be slightly different on the building.

FACTS
Orange stars highlight interesting facts about the building or activity.

ASK the ARCHITECT!
Inside the orange protractor look for basic facts about architecture and design.

LOOK UP!
Describes the drawing activity for each building.

On the left hand side, you will find the name of the building, an architectural drawing and facts about its architecture and style.

The right hand page has a drawing activity for each building plus other fun facts.

COLOR, DRAW AND SKETCH!

THE MAP
Each walk begins with a map. The map shows the name and address of each building as well as any other items of interest- like the closest subway stop.

TIME
Walks are designed to take about one hour. Do the whole walk or just a few buildings.

GLOSSARY
In the back of the book you will find a glossary of terms and architecture styles.

Note from the Author

As an architect in New York, I am in love with the buildings and landscape of this city. When my children started school, I began giving tours of the local neighborhoods to their classmates and teachers. Pretty soon we had big groups of kids and grownups talking about architecture and the local buildings. We discussed shapes and building styles and practiced drawing some of the designs and concepts we observed. The idea was such a hit that many parents, teachers and colleagues encouraged me to share the walks on a larger scale. This is how **LOOK UP!** was born.

Through these walks, you get an introduction to architecture and a new appreciation of the local neighborhoods. The walks are easy to follow and designed to be enjoyed as a history lesson, a sketchbook or a fun way to spend a day. When you look up you can find all kinds of interesting clues to the history of the neighborhood and the city. How were the buildings built? What materials did they use and why? What is important about this building? What kind of architecture defines a neighborhood?

I love experiencing architecture through the eyes of others. I can't wait to see you passing by on your architecture walk. I hope I catch you looking up!

WELCOME TO NEW YORK CITY!

Some of the most famous buildings in the world are here. New York City is made up of five boroughs:

Manhattan

Brooklyn

Queens

Staten Island

The Bronx

Each borough is made up of different neighborhoods. Every neighborhood in the city is unique.

The architecture tells a story. It gives us clues about the people who lived and worked there, the architects who designed the buildings, and the people who built them.

UPPER WEST SIDE WALK

The Upper West Side has been around for over 300 years. It wasn't always as popular as it is today. The area was all woodlands and the downtowners called it "The Wilderness!"

This walk begins at the famous Dakota Building and ends at the American Museum of Natural History. On the way you will see some famous New York apartment buildings and one of the city's oldest churches. There is plenty to do inside the museum or across the street in Central Park. After your walk, try a warm pretzel and sketch in your book!

Ⓑ Ⓒ SUBWAY

UPPER EAST SIDE WALK

The Upper East Side is the neighborhood on the other side of Central Park. The UES walk will take you along Fifth Avenue.

You can start this walk at either end. You could go to the Central Park Zoo or have tea at the Plaza Hotel. The buildings on the Upper East Side are very elegant. They used a lot of limestone, copper, and other expensive materials. Have a look at the fountain and the sculptures in Grand Army Plaza too. They are highlighted on your map.

④ ⑤ ⑥ SUBWAY

FLATIRON WALK

This is Madison Square Park and the home of the famous Flatiron Building. In fact the whole neighborhood is called the Flatiron District because the building is so popular. There are lots of other great buildings surrounding the park. Madison Square Park is also known for the different art installations that it displays.

Ⓝ Ⓡ Ⓠ SUBWAY

BRYANT PARK WALK

On the Bryant Park walk, you will see the world famous New York Public Library building. If you have time, you should walk through the inside- it's just as impressive as the outside.

You will also be checking out a few different types of skyscrapers. You will see what happens when old buildings run into new buildings and how architects combine different styles of design. After you finish your walk, you can relax in the park, grab some lunch and sketch.

Ⓝ Ⓡ Ⓠ Ⓑ Ⓓ Ⓕ Ⓜ ⑦ SUBWAY

BRONX

MANHATTAN

QUEENS

BROOKLYN

LOOK UP! TABLE of CONTENTS

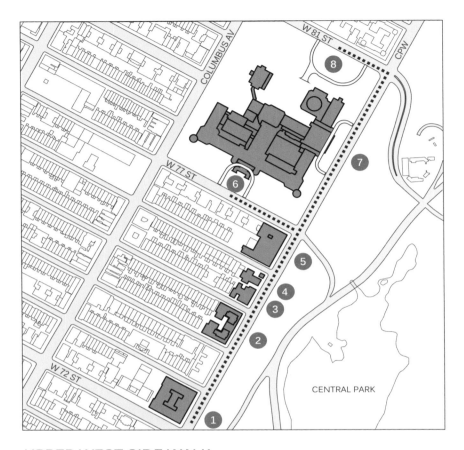

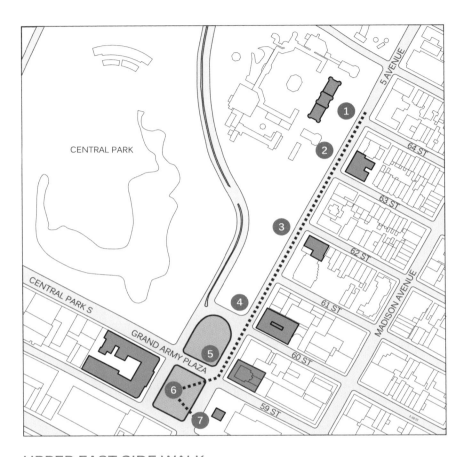

UPPER WEST SIDE WALK

1 **The Dakota Building:** 1 West 72nd Street — 4

2 **San Remo Building:** 145-146 Central Park West — 6

3 **Kenilworth Building:** 151 Central Park West — 8

4 **Universalist Church:** 160 Central Park West — 10

5 **New York Historical Society:** 170 Central Park West — 12

6 **American Museum of Natural History:** Central Park West @ 77th St. — 14

7 **American Museum of Natural History:** Central Park West @ 78th St. — 16

8 **Rose Center for Earth & Space:** Central Park West @ 81st Street — 18

UPPER EAST SIDE WALK

1 **Arsenal Building:** 821 Fifth Avenue @ 64th Street — 22

2 **820 Fifth Avenue:** 820 Fifth Avenue @ 63rd Street — 24

3 **The Knickerbocker Club:** 2 East 62nd Street — 26

4 **The Metropolitan Club:** 11-11 East 60th Street — 28

5 **The Sherry Netherland Hotel:** 781 Fifth Avenue — 30

6 **The Plaza Hotel:** 768 Fifth Avenue — 32

7 **The Apple Store:** 767 Fifth Avenue — 34

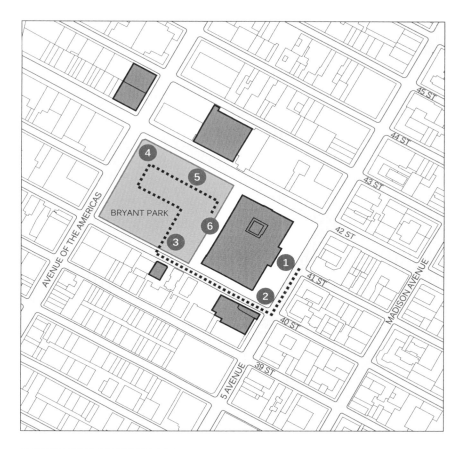

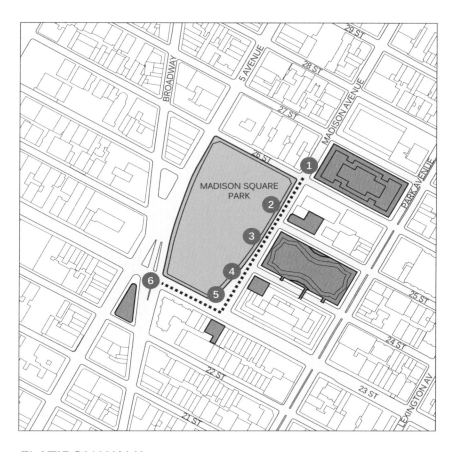

BRYANT PARK WALK

1 The New York Public Library Building: 38
Fifth Avenue @ 42nd Street (front facade)

2 HSBC Bank Building/Knox Hat Building: 40
452 Fifth Avenue

3 Bryant Park Hotel: 40 West 40th Street   42

4 Bank of America: 1 Bryant Park   44

5 The W. R. Grace Building: 1114 Sixth Avenue   46

6 The New York Public Library Building: 48
Fifth Avenue @ 42nd Street (back facade)

FLATIRON WALK

1 New York Life Insurance Building: 51 Madison Avenue   52

2 Appellate Division of the Supreme Court of the   54
State of New York: 35 East 25th Street

3 Metropolitan Life North Building: 56
11-25 Madison Avenue

4 Met Life Tower: 58
SE Corner of Madison Avenue and 24th Street

5 One Madison Park: One Madison Avenue   60

6 The Flatiron Building: 175 Fifth Avenue   62

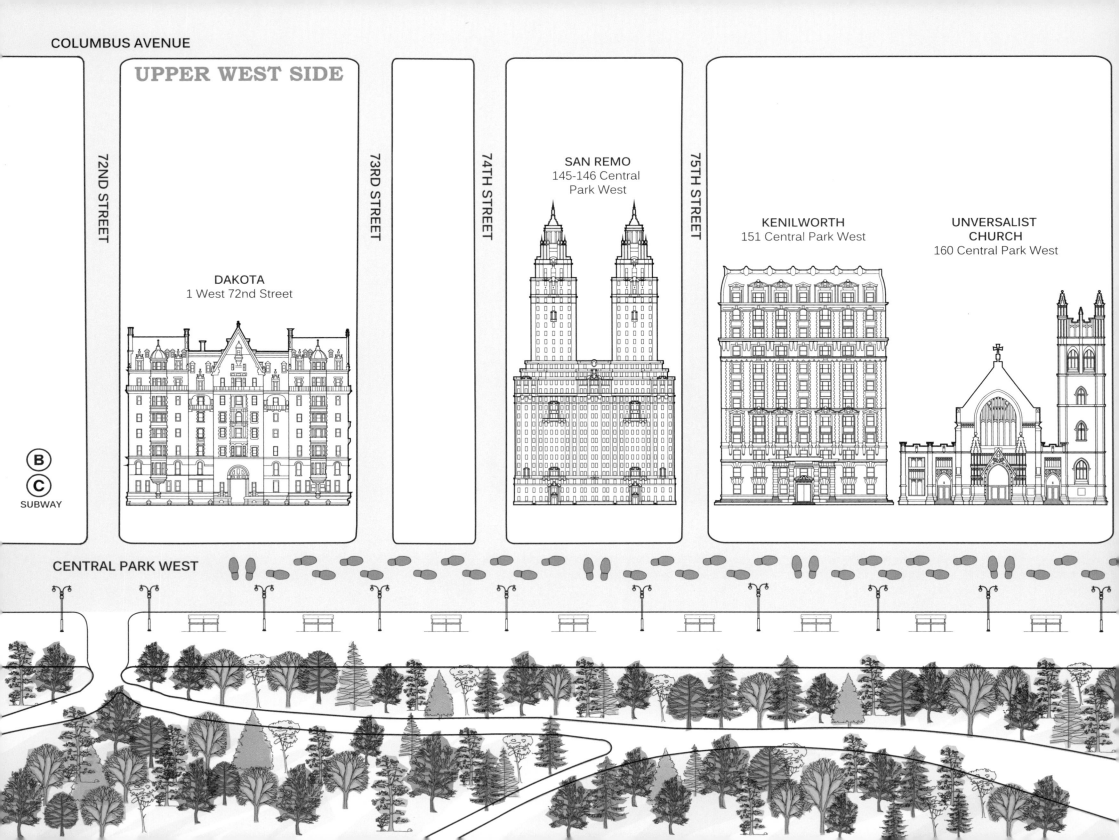

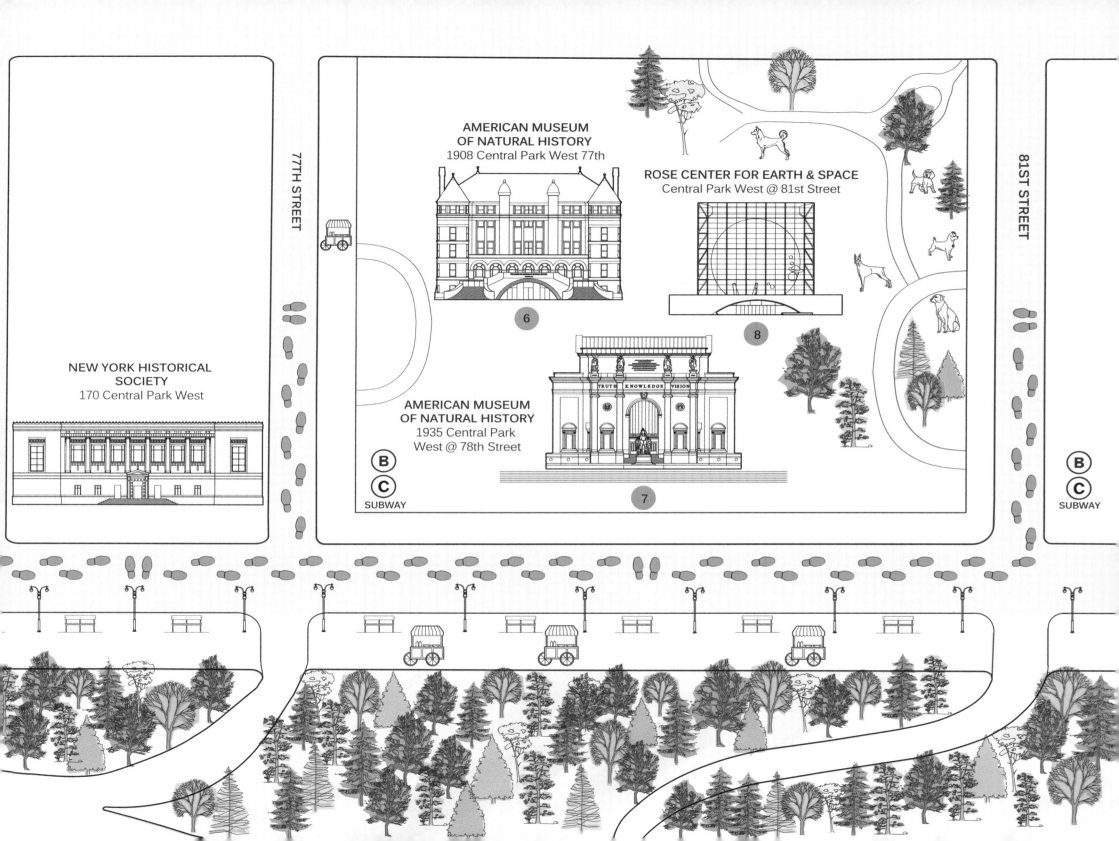

77TH STREET

81ST STREET

AMERICAN MUSEUM OF NATURAL HISTORY
1908 Central Park West 77th

ROSE CENTER FOR EARTH & SPACE
Central Park West @ 81st Street

6

8

NEW YORK HISTORICAL SOCIETY
170 Central Park West

AMERICAN MUSEUM OF NATURAL HISTORY
1935 Central Park West @ 78th Street

TRUTH KNOWLEDGE VISION

(B)
(C)
SUBWAY

7

(B)
(C)
SUBWAY

THE DAKOTA BUILDING

The Dakota was the first luxury apartment building in New York City and the first to have an elevator.

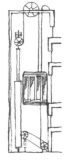

The Dakota is nine stories high. Before the elevator, buildings were usually six stories because people refused to walk any higher.

Year Built
1884
Architect
Henry J. Hardenbergh
Style
Renaissance
Materials
Limestone, Brick

Why is the roof turquoise? It's made of copper.

When copper is exposed to air and water for a long time, it changes color: copper to gray to turquoise.

A Dakota Native American sculpture keeps watch above the 72nd Street entrance. Edward Clark, the building developer, loved Western names.

Many famous people have lived in the Dakota Building. It is best known as the home of John Lennon from the Beatles, who was shot outside the entrance.

Building Blocks

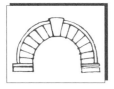
ARCH

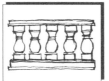
BALUSTRADE

BAY WINDOW

CHIMNEY

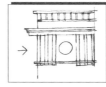
DORMER

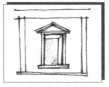
FRIEZE

NICHE

PITCHED ROOF

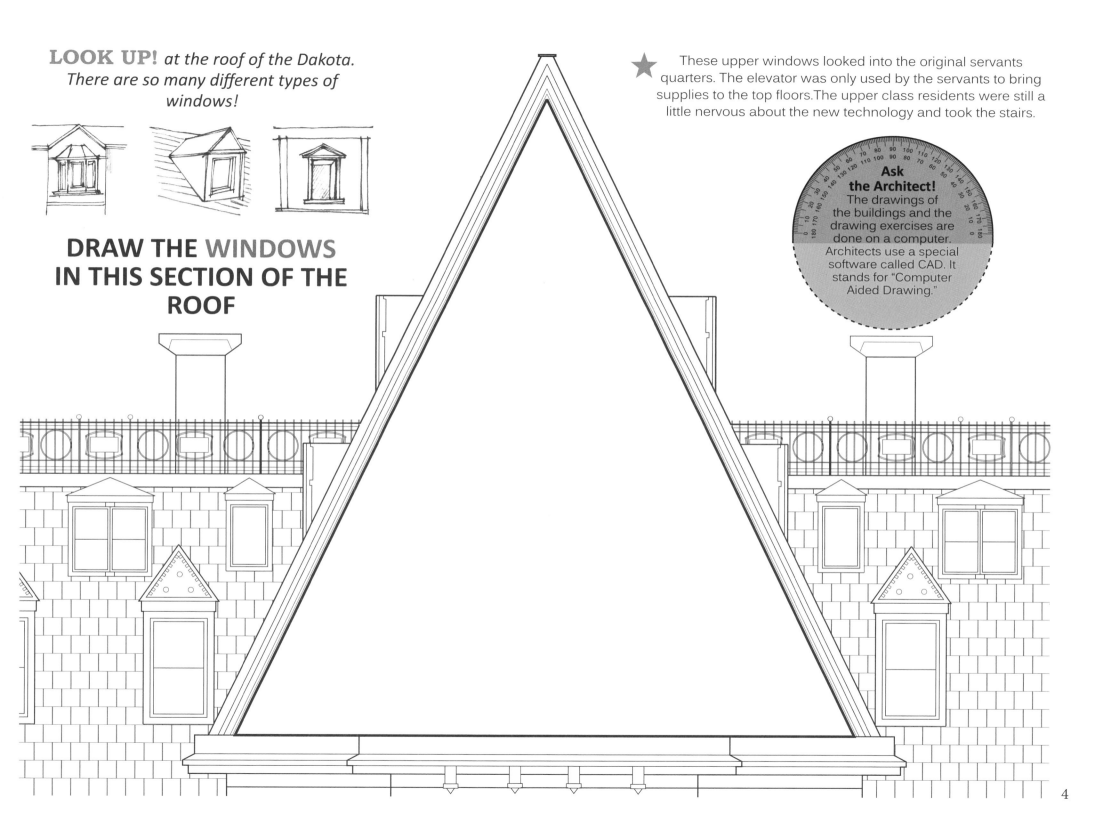

LOOK UP! *at the roof of the Dakota. There are so many different types of windows!*

DRAW THE WINDOWS IN THIS SECTION OF THE ROOF

These upper windows looked into the original servants quarters. The elevator was only used by the servants to bring supplies to the top floors. The upper class residents were still a little nervous about the new technology and took the stairs.

Ask the Architect! The drawings of the buildings and the drawing exercises are done on a computer. Architects use a special software called CAD. It stands for "Computer Aided Drawing."

4

THE SAN REMO BUILDING

The San Remo, like many buildings, is created by stacking shapes. There is a base, middle and top. Basic shapes become the building blocks architects use to design a building.

The San Remo has a block shaped base and middle. The top are two tall rectangular towers. The towers are topped by two elegant crowns. These crowns hide water tanks on the roof.

Year Built
1930
Architect
Emery Roth
Style
Neo Classical/
Art Deco
Materials
Steel, Limestone,
Brick

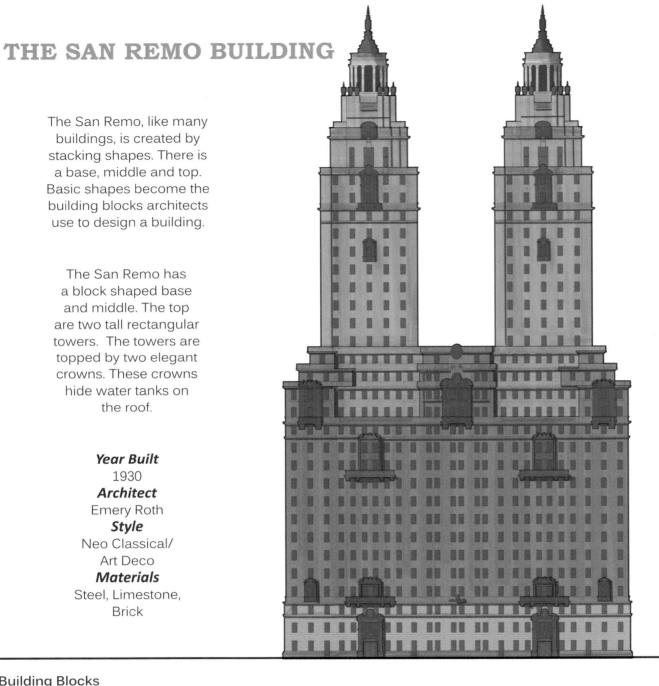

The **twin towers** of the San Remo are the first set ever built in New York City. The design allows more light and fresh air to reach the street.

Twin towers have been used in many New York buildings. The most famous examples in NYC are the pre-9/11 World Trade Center and the Time Warner Center.

The San Remo is a **Neo-Classic** ("new" classic) architectural design. The style is inspired by the building styles of Greece and Rome.

One of the most important ideas in Classical Architecture is **symmetry**. Symmetry is another word for balanced. In architecture, it means both sides are exactly the same.

symmetrical

asymmetrical

Building Blocks

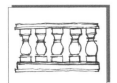

BALUSTRADE

BRACKET

BROKEN ARCH

CARTOUCHE

CUPOLA

ENTRANCE

PEDIMENT

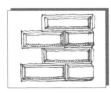

RUSTICATED STONE

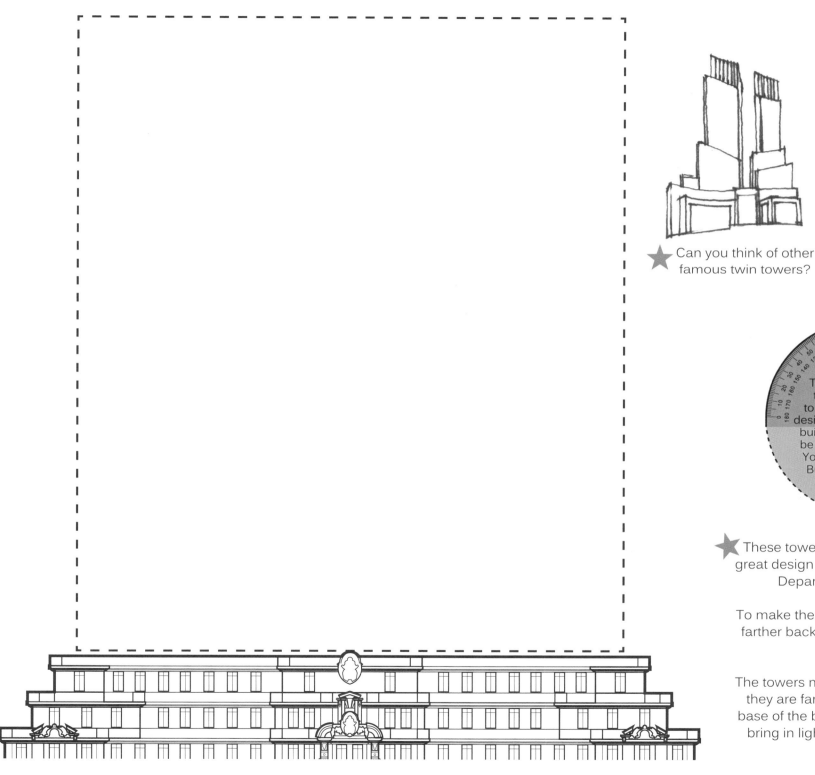

LOOK UP! *at the San Remo's Twin Towers. You can't see the details from the street. Imagine what they might look like.*

★ Can you think of other famous twin towers?

DRAW YOUR OWN SET OF TWIN TOWERS IN THE DOTTED LINES

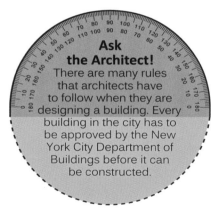

Ask the Architect! There are many rules that architects have to follow when they are designing a building. Every building in the city has to be approved by the New York City Department of Buildings before it can be constructed.

★ These towers are a perfect example of a great design that was a response to a NYC Department of Buildings rule.

To make the building taller, it had to be set farther back from the street to let in more air and light.

The towers meet the requirement because they are farther from the street than the base of the building. Two seperate towers bring in light and air from all four sides. ★

THE KENILWORTH BUILDING

There are many ways of making a building unique. It could have an interesting shape or it could be dressed up with decorative design elements.

The Kenilworth has a simple shape but many layers of decoration. Architects call this **ornamentation.**

The design is balanced or "symmetrical" like the Classical style but it has more elaborate ornamentation.

Year Built
1908
Architect
Townsend, Steile, Haskell
Style
French Second Empire (Victorian Style)
Materials
Limestone, Brick

The Kenilworth Building is sometimes called **The Wedding Cake Building.** Layers of red brick with limestone frosting. Just like a wedding cake, it has swirls of frosting and flowers. The Kenilworth is decorated with swags, cartouches (*car-toosh*), brackets, and quoins (*coins*).

The columns around the beautiful entrance of the Kenilworth are called **banded columns.** Stone discs break up the column like bands...or layers on a cake!

Look around the base of the Kenilworth. Like many apartment buildings it is surrounded by a "dry moat." A moat is a ditch or trench that surrounds a building. They were used to defend buildings like castles and could be filled with water or dry and lined with wooden spikes.

In a New York City apartment buildings, a dry moat allows light and fresh air into the basement.

Building Blocks

BRACKET

BROKEN ARCH

CARTOUCHE

COLUMNS

PEDIMENT

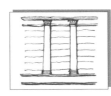
PILASTER

QUOINS

SWAG

LOOK UP! *at the Kenilworth. This window shows a circular cartouche over the window.*

★ A **cartouche** is a circular stone emblem. Sometimes it contains the image of a person, the name of a king or queen, an inscription or a date.

DESIGN YOUR OWN CARTOUCHE FOR THE WINDOW

USE YOUR IMAGINATION TO DESIGN A SPECIAL SYMBOL, CHARACTER, OR SAYING

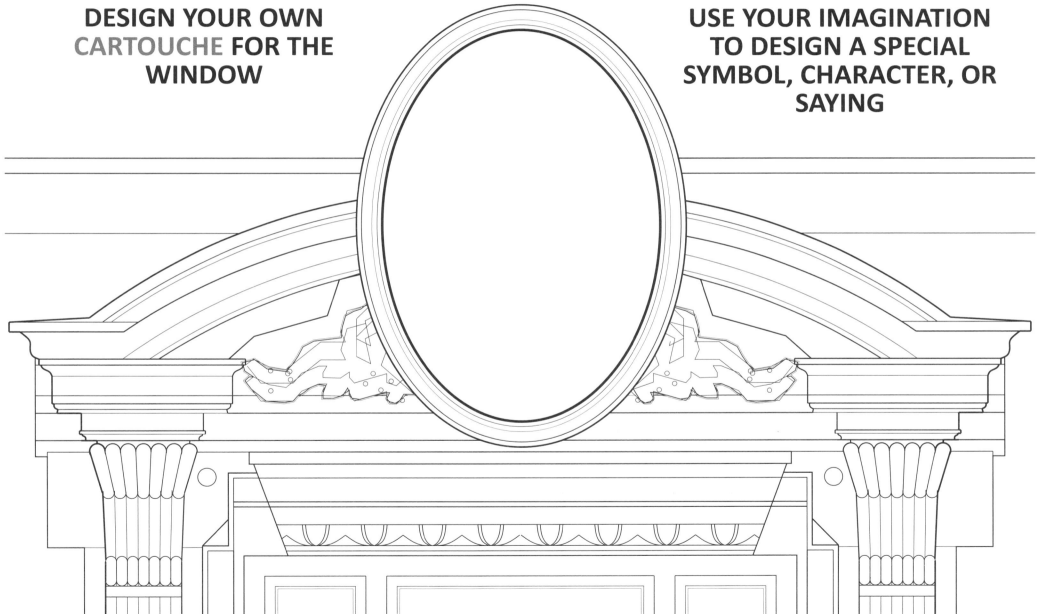

THE UNIVERSALIST CHURCH

What's different about this building?
It's a style you haven't seen yet called **Gothic**.
It stands out on the street between its Classical architecture neighbors.

Before the arrival of Gothic Style, many buildings in Europe were dreary. They were dark, cold and damp. The buttresses and pointed arches of Gothic Architecture allowed architects to build higher. This opened up the spaces for sunlight and fresh air.

Year Built
1898
Architect
William Appleton Potter
Style
NeoGothic ("new" gothic)
Materials
Limestone, Slate

Gothic Architecture
Churches and University Buildings
Asymmetrical and heavily decorated
Triggers emotion and imagination

VS

Classical Architecture
Public and Commercial Buildings
Orderly and symmetrical
Triggers logic and reason

Do these Building Blocks remind you of anything?
Many of these shapes were also used to design castles

Gothic structures are taller, more open, more decorative and flooded with light and air. They are inspiring. No wonder this style is popular for churches, castles, and universities.

Building Blocks

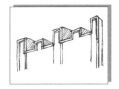
BATTLEMENT

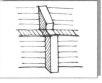
BUTTRESS

LANCET

PITCHED ROOF

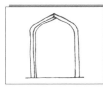
POINTED ARCH

QUATREFOIL

SPIRE

TRACERY

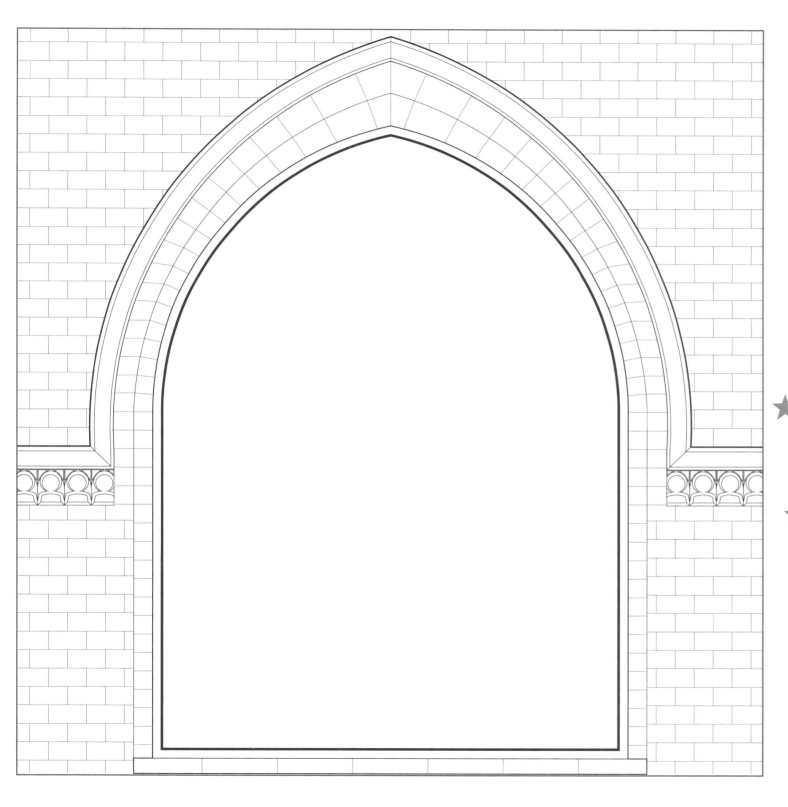

LOOK UP! *at the stained glass windows of the Church.*

DESIGN YOUR OWN STAINED GLASS WINDOW

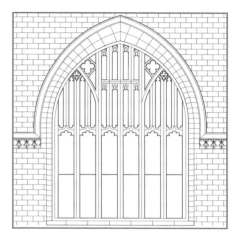

★ The church's alter is designed by Louis Comfort Tiffany, an artist famous for his stained glass lamps. His father was the founder of New York's most well-known jewelry store, Tiffany and Company.

★ Both PT Barnum, the circus owner, and Lou Gehrig, the famous baseball player, were members of this church.

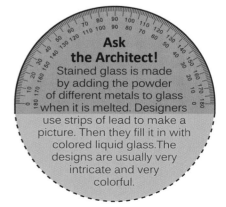

Ask the Architect! Stained glass is made by adding the powder of different metals to glass when it is melted. Designers use strips of lead to make a picture. Then they fill it in with colored liquid glass. The designs are usually very intricate and very colorful.

THE NEW YORK HISTORICAL SOCIETY

Year Built
1908
Architect
York & Sawyer
(North/South Wings 1938 by
Walker and Gillette)
Style
NeoClassical/Beaux Arts
Materials
Limestone, Copper Roof

The New York Historical Society building is a perfect example of symmetry. Symmetry means both sides are exactly the same.

It models the temples built in Ancient Greece with its repeated, even columns and simple ornamentation.

A common decoration used in Classical Greek Architecture is a carved pattern called a **key pattern**

Can you find it on the building?

Sometimes they looked like a maze or a labyrinth like the one on the NY Historical Society. Others were ocean themed like waves or seashells.

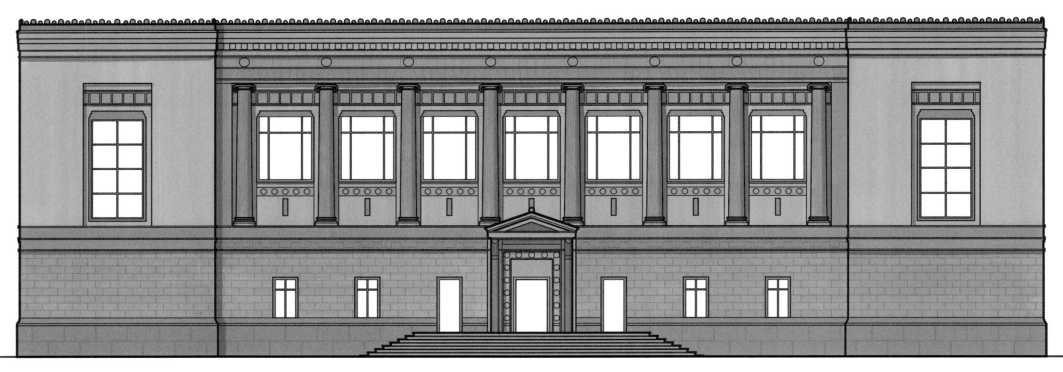

Building Blocks

BRACKET

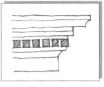

DENTIL
MOULDING

ENTRY

FRIEZE

IONIC COLUMN

KEY PATTERN

PEDIMENT

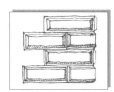

RUSTICATED
STONE

New York City has an amazing history! That is the specialty of this museum and library. They even have original architectural drawings from famous city architects.

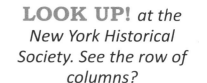

LOOK UP! *at the New York Historical Society. See the row of columns?*

⭐ *There are three major types of columns used in classical architecture.*

DORIC COLUMN
A simple column without a base. It has a plain flat top.

IONIC COLUMN
A taller, skinnier column. The base is large and looks like stacked rings. The top or "capital" is decorated like a scroll.

CORINTHIAN COLUMN
The tallest and most decorative column. It has a larger base and the capital is carved with leaves and scrolls.

DESIGN YOUR OWN
COLUMN

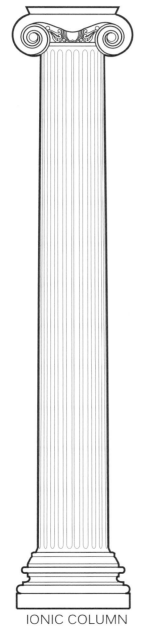

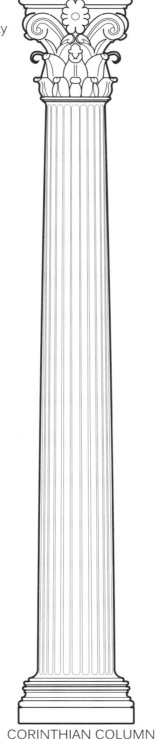

DORIC COLUMN   IONIC COLUMN   CORINTHIAN COLUMN   YOUR COLUMN

THE AMERICAN MUSEUM OF NATURAL HISTORY 77th Street

The 77th Street entrance to the American Museum of Natural History is extremely long. The length of the building is a whole city block!

Year Built
1908
Architect
Cady, Berg and See
Style
NeoRomanesque
Materials
Rusticated Pink Brownstone, Granite, Slate

The texture of the construction materials is one way to add interest to a building.

Curved and slanted lines and textured stone are different and fun to look at.

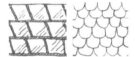

You can also repeat shapes. This building has a lot of semi-circles and curves.

The arches, arcade, conical roof, the domes, even the low wall along the stairs are all curved.

Building Blocks

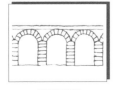

ARCADE

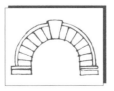

ARCH

BALUSTRADE

CONICAL ROOF

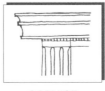

CORNICE

CUPOLA

HIPPED ROOF

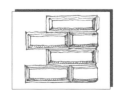

RUSTICATED STONE

LOOK UP! *at the American Museum of Natural History.*

DRAW THE BUSY ENTRANCE TO THE MUSEUM
VISITORS COMING AND GOING, INTERESTING ARTIFACTS BEING DELIVERED

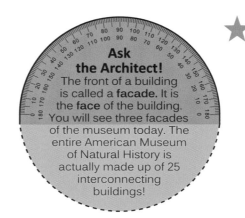

Ask the Architect!
The front of a building is called a **facade**. It is the **face** of the building. You will see three facades of the museum today. The entire American Museum of Natural History is actually made up of 25 interconnecting buildings!

Historically, horses and carriages entered through the big central arch. People went through the row of smaller arches above. A row of arches is called an **arcade**.

Scientific studies have shown that human beings instinctively prefer curves to straight lines.

Can you find all the curves in this drawing?

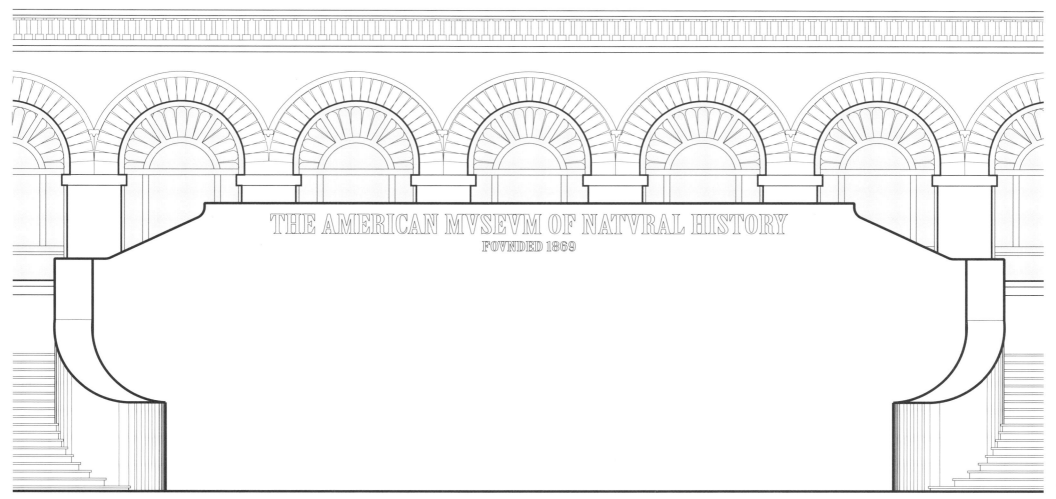

THE AMERICAN MVSEVM OF NATVRAL HISTORY
FOVNDED 1869

Some parts of a building are designed to decorate or to tell a story or to give us an idea of what we will see inside.

The Central Park West entrance to the museum does all three.

TRUTH
KNOWLEDGE
VISION
carved right into the stone!

Year Built
1935
Architect
Trowbridge and Livingston, John Russell Pope (Theodore Roosevelt Memorial)
Style
Beaux Arts
Materials
Granite

The sculptures at the top are all important American explorers: Daniel Boone, John James Audobon, William Lewis and Meriwether Clark.

The museum displays and preserves what these brave explorers discovered on their adventures.

This entrance is dedicated to Theodore Roosevelt, our 26th president, shown here on his horse. He was passionate about nature and exploration. He even donated two of the elephants inside.

The frieze shows all kinds of animals just like the exhibits you'll see in the museum.

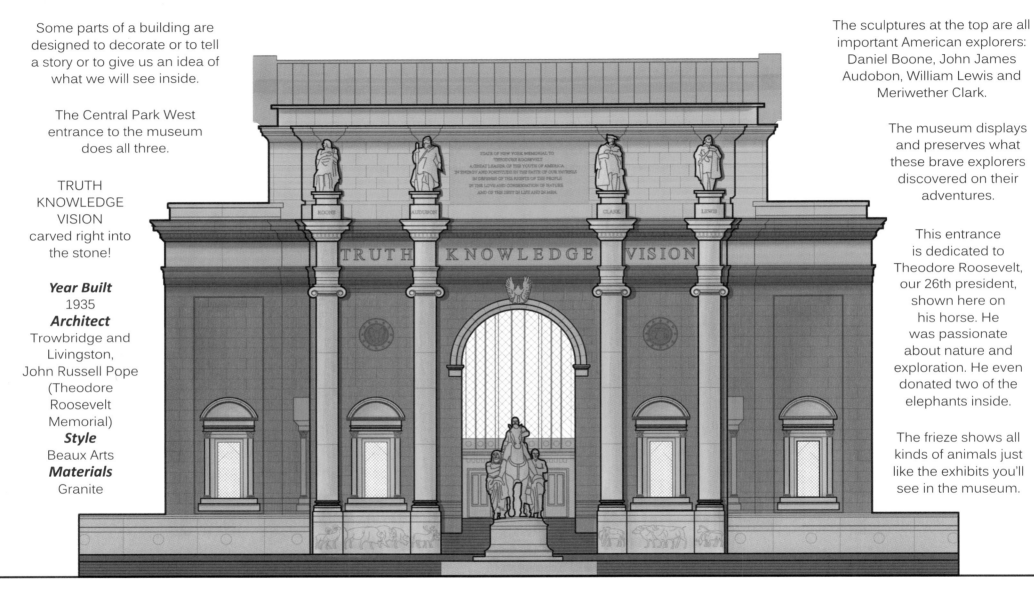

Building Blocks

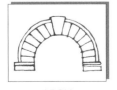

ARCH

CORINTHIAN COLUMN

CORNICE

ENTRY

DECORATIVE FRIEZE

IONIC COLUMN

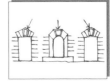

KEYSTONE

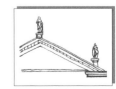

SCULPTURE

LOOK UP! *at the sculpture and carvings of the American Museum of Natural History. The outside of the museum tells us a lot about the building.*

DRAW YOUR OWN
SCULPTURE
ON THE CAPITALS OF THE COLUMNS
DO THEY TELL A STORY ABOUT YOU?

Just inside the doors, get inspired by the writings of Teddy Roosevelt and see the largest freestanding dinosaur display in the world!

The American Museum of Natural History is said to contain over 30 million specimens of plants, animals, humans, fossils, minerals, rocks, meteorites, and human cultural artifacts.

The museum's first exhibits were displayed in the Arsenal Building on Fifth Avenue which you will see on the Upper East Side Walk.

THE ROSE CENTER FOR EARTH AND SPACE and THE HAYDEN PLANETARIUM

Modern Architecture is very different from the other styles you have seen so far.

Do you like the Modern style? Which style of architecture is your favorite?

The glass cube is six stories high. You can count the stories on the steel grid.

The sphere in the center of the glass cube weighs 2000 tons and has the Hayden Planetarium inside.

This style was inspired by advances in technology and building techniques. Glass could be used for more than just windows and why hide the steel beams? They're pretty cool to see.

The Modern style takes away all the details of a traditional building. The style comes from the building materials, the building structure and how it's made.

STEEL BEAM

Year Built
2000
Architect
Polshek Partners
Style
Modern
Materials
Steel, Glass, Copper, Stone

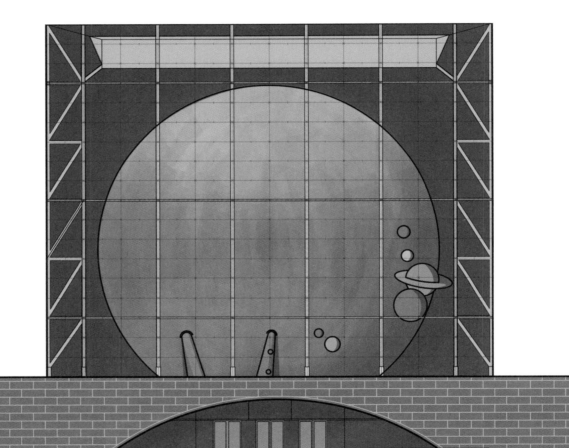

A planetarium is a building where you can see a model of the solar system. Here, you can see stars, planets and moons inside and out.

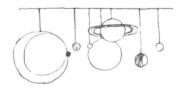

Building Blocks

ARCH

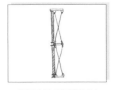

CABLE SYSTEM

CUBE

CURTAIN WALL

GLASS FINS

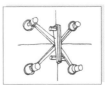

GLASS SPIDER CONNECTION

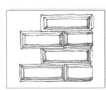

RUSTICATED STONE

TRUSS

⭐ Architect, James Stewart Polshek described the design for the Rose Center as a "cosmic cathedral." How would you describe it?

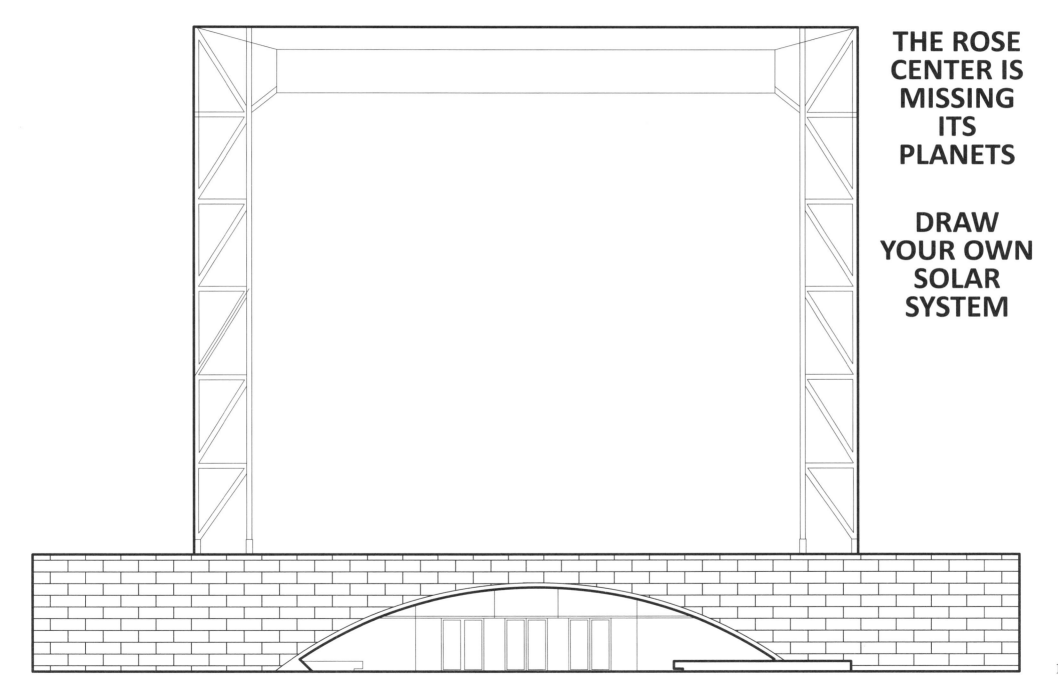

THE ROSE CENTER IS MISSING ITS PLANETS

DRAW YOUR OWN SOLAR SYSTEM

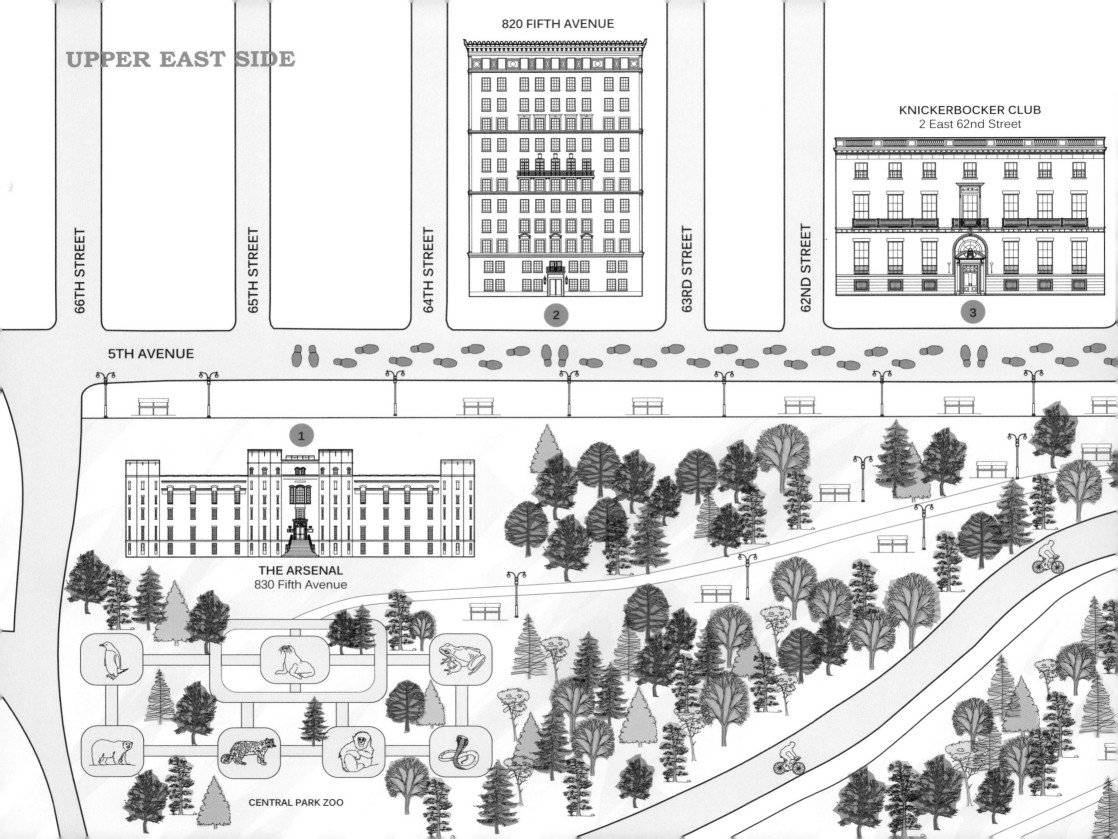

UPPER EAST SIDE

820 FIFTH AVENUE

KNICKERBOCKER CLUB
2 East 62nd Street

66TH STREET

65TH STREET

64TH STREET

63RD STREET

62ND STREET

2

3

5TH AVENUE

1

THE ARSENAL
830 Fifth Avenue

CENTRAL PARK ZOO

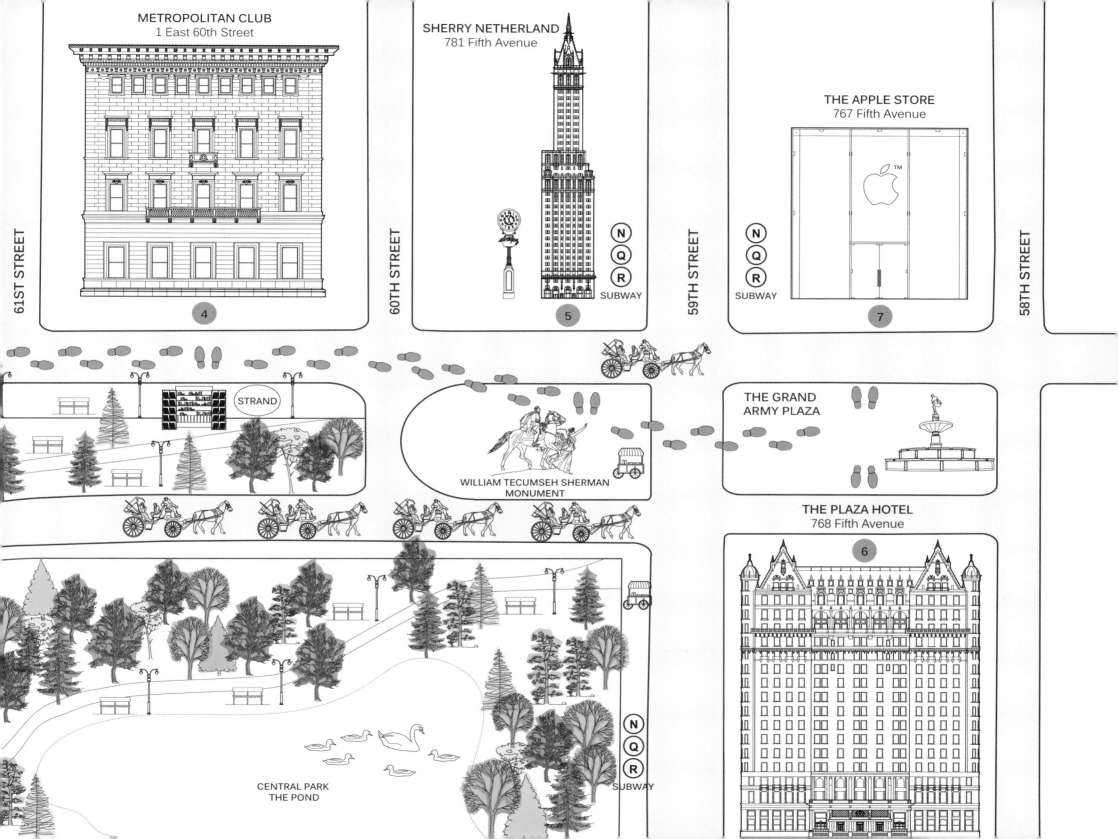

METROPOLITAN CLUB
1 East 60th Street

4

SHERRY NETHERLAND
781 Fifth Avenue

Ⓝ Ⓠ Ⓡ SUBWAY

5

THE APPLE STORE
767 Fifth Avenue

Ⓝ Ⓠ Ⓡ SUBWAY

7

61ST STREET

60TH STREET

59TH STREET

58TH STREET

STRAND

WILLIAM TECUMSEH SHERMAN
MONUMENT

THE GRAND
ARMY PLAZA

THE PLAZA HOTEL
768 Fifth Avenue

6

Ⓝ Ⓠ Ⓡ SUBWAY

CENTRAL PARK
THE POND

THE ARSENAL BUILDING

Year Built
1848
Architect
Martin E. Thompson
Style
Neo Gothic
Materials
Brick, Limestone

Does the Arsenal Building remind you of anything? Maybe a medieval fortress? It was originally built to store weapons and ammunition for the New York State Militia.

It was only used as an arsenal for a short time. After 1935 the details of the rifle stair rail, drum lights, and crossed swords were added at the entrance to honor the building's history.

Ways to defend the building are designed right into the structure. This is sometimes called military or "defensive" architecture.

Turrets: allow enemies to be seen approaching from far away.

Battlements: allow archers to defend the building from the roof.

Slotted windows: allow arrows to be fired out while the marksman stays under cover.

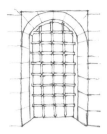

Other features of defensive architecture are inner and outer stone walls, moats that surround a building with water, and iron gates at the main entrance.

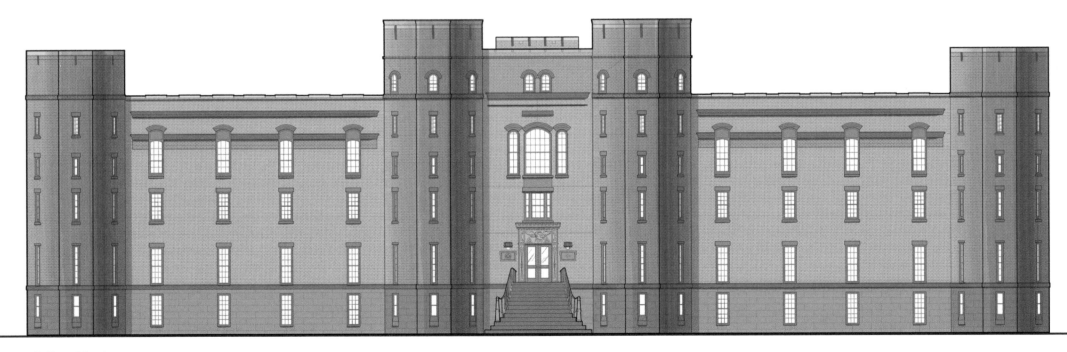

Building Blocks

ARCHED WINDOW

BATTLEMENT

PALADIAN WINDOW

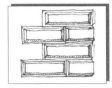

RUSTICATED STONE

SASH WINDOW

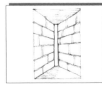

SLOT WINDOW "ARROW SLIT"

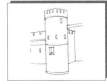

TURRET

WINDOW HEADER

FIND AND COLOR THE MILITARY ELEMENTS ON THE ARSENAL ENTRY

★ A cast iron American eagle guards the entrance. The American eagle has been our national symbol since 1782 and is a featured decoration on many government buildings.

★ B. Waterhouse Hawkins, paleontologist, had a special studio in the Arsenal Building to reconstruct dinosaur skeletons for the American Museum of Natural History.

★ In the early 1900s during a restoration, a secret passage and underground spring were discovered underneath the building!

820 FIFTH AVENUE

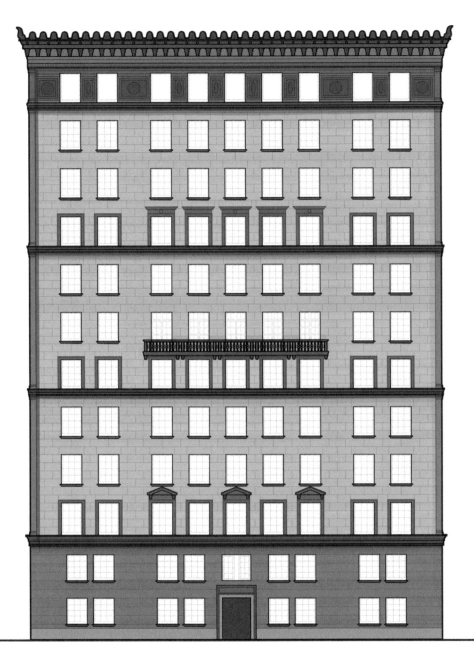

820 Fifth Avenue is built in the Italian Renaissance Palazzo style. The Palazzo style of architecture is based on palaces (palazzos) built by wealthy families during the Italian Renaissance.

The style fits right in on Fifth Avenue. This stretch is called "The Gold Coast" because some of the most exclusive apartment buildings and hotels are here.

Year Built
1916
Architect
Starett & van Vleck
Style
Italian Renaissance
Materials
Limestone, Copper

Upper class New Yorkers didn't live in apartment buildings until the early 1900s. Most lived in private mansions. Many of these mansions only stood for 20-30 years before they were demolished to make way for the new apartment buildings.

One mansion had 121 rooms, 31 bathrooms, and a private underground railway system to deliver coal to heat the house!

What makes 820 Fifth Avenue so elegant? The smooth limestone facade (the "face" of the building), long slender pilasters at each corner, neat rows of windows and the carved antefixes, swags and moldings give it a grand look.

Building Blocks

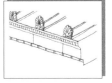

ANTEFIX

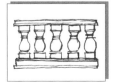

BALUSTRADE

CARTOUCHE

CORNICE

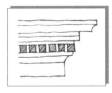

DENTIL MOULDING

PEDIMENT

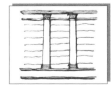

PILASTER

SWAG

LOOK UP! *at the roof of 820 Fifth Avenue.*

DESIGN NEW SYMBOLS TO FILL THE ANTEFIXES FOR THE ROOF OF THE BUILDING

They can be carved faces, flowers, seashells, shapes, anything you can imagine

An **antefix** is a carved ornament that sticks up at the end of a row of roof tiles to hide the joint where the tiles meet the roof. You can see antefixes inside the Metropolitan Museum of Art that date back to 500 BC.

Some **antefixes** are carved out of stone. These are made with copper. If you went on the Upper West Side Walk, you might remember what happens to copper when it is exposed to air and water. It changes color. Copper to gray to the turquiose color you see on the roof of 820 Fifth Avenue.

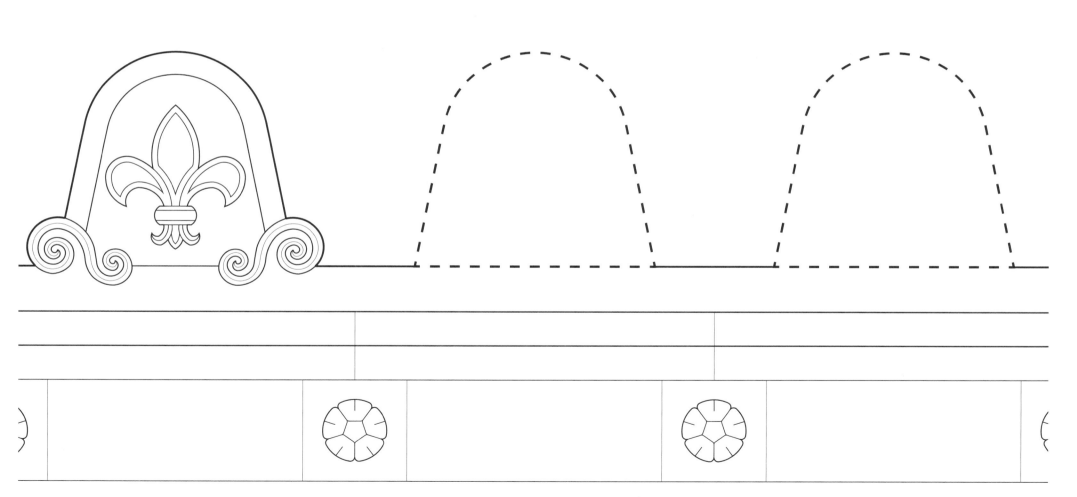

THE KNICKERBOCKER CLUB

The Knickerbocker Club looks more like the type of homes that once lined Fifth Avenue.

What exactly is a Knickerbocker? A Knickerbocker refers to a New Yorker who can trace their ancestry back to the original Dutch settlers who founded New York City in the 1600s.

Knickerbocker refers to the type of pants they wore. They were gathered just under their knees. The name of our basketball team, the New York Knicks, comes from the word Knickerbocker.

Famous members of The Knickerbocker Club include John Jacob Astor and Franklin Delano Roosevelt. Even the architects of the building were members of Knickerbocker families.

It is a combination of different architectural styles but looks a lot like an early American upper class home. Conservative, symmetrical, three-story and rectangular with multi-pane windows.

Year Built
1915
Architect
Delano & Aldrich
Style
Colonial Revival
Materials
Limestone, Brick

One of the most interesting decorative elements of this building is the ornamental ironwork. Examples of beautiful ironwork can be seen all over the city.

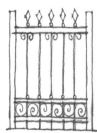

Building Blocks

ARCHED WINDOW

BALCONY

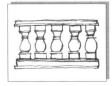
BALUSTRADE

BRACKET

BROKEN ARCH

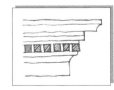
DENTIL MOULDING

SASH WINDOW

WINDOW HEADER

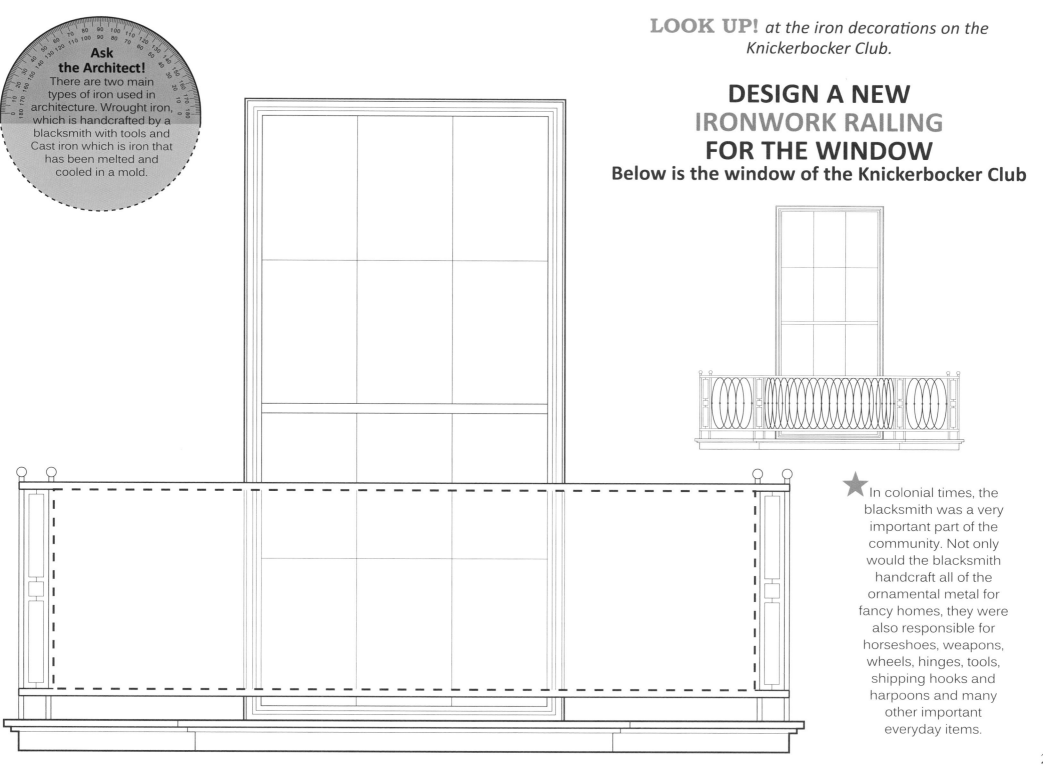

Ask the Architect!
There are two main types of iron used in architecture. Wrought iron, which is handcrafted by a blacksmith with tools and Cast iron which is iron that has been melted and cooled in a mold.

DESIGN A NEW
IRONWORK RAILING
FOR THE WINDOW
Below is the window of the Knickerbocker Club

In colonial times, the blacksmith was a very important part of the community. Not only would the blacksmith handcraft all of the ornamental metal for fancy homes, they were also responsible for horseshoes, weapons, wheels, hinges, tools, shipping hooks and harpoons and many other important everyday items.

THE METROPOLITAN CLUB

The Metropolitan Club is another Palazzo style building. This one is even more extravagant than 820 Fifth Avenue. It has beautiful carved decoration and a giant cornice.
The cornice extends six feet from the building wall.

Like the Knickerbocker, the Metropolitan is a private social club. It was started by J.P. Morgan, the famous financier, in 1891.

Year Built
1894/1912 East Wing
Architect
McKim, Mead & White
East Wing by Ogden Codman Jr.
Style
Italian Renaissance
Materials
Limestone, Copper

Cornice is the Italian word for "ledge." It is a horizontal ledge that projects from the building just under the roof line. Cornices are often carved in great detail for decoration like the one you see here. They also help protect the building walls from the effects of rain, snow, and ice.

You can see other types of cornices inside buildings.

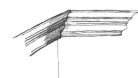

They can be a decorative moulding just under the ceiling

Or a ledge over a door or window

Building Blocks

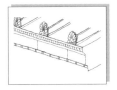

ANTEFIX

BALUSTRADE

BRACKET

CORNICE

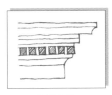

DENTIL MOULDING

EGG & DART MOULDING

FRIEZE

QUOINS

LOOK UP! *at the carved moldings under the cornice on the Metropolitan Club.*
There are several different designs: **egg & dart**, **dentil** *and a* **flower** *pattern.*

DESIGN YOUR OWN PATTERN TO DECORATE THE BUILDING

Look at the floral pattern on the Metropolitan Club
Use your imagination
to create an interesting pattern

Ask the Architect! Limestone has been used in architecture for over 5000 years. In addition to being beautiful to look at, it is smooth and durable and perfect for carved decorative elements.

★ Egg and dart and dentil molding are traditional moldings used in Classical Greek and Roman architecture. You will see them on many buildings in New York and all over the world. The other carved moldings like the flowers you see on this building, are specifically designed for this building and give it a unique look.

THE SHERRY NETHERLAND HOTEL

Gargoyles!
The Sherry Netherland is a Gothic skyscraper complete with mysterious dark brick, griffin lanterns, and a needle-pointed copper spire jutting into the sky.

Although it may not seem very tall compared to some of New York's newer buildings, The Sherry Netherland was the tallest apartment hotel in the city when it was built in 1927 and one of the first steel framed buildings.

Year Built
1927
Architect
Schultze & Weaver and Buchman & Kahn
Style
Gothic
French Renaissance
Materials
Brick, Copper

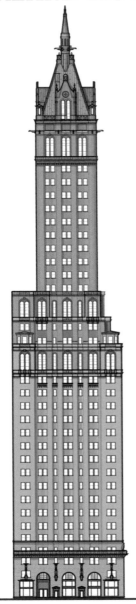

During construction of the Sherry Netherland, a terrible fire broke out on the wooden scaffolding around the tower. Firefighters had to find new ways to fight fires on such tall buildings. They started by changing the scaffolding frames from wood to metal.

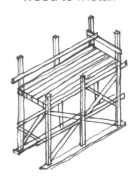

Many gargoyles were designed to preserve the walls and foundations of a building by draining rainwater away from the surface.

When gutters were invented, architects still used gargoyles as decoration. People believed the gargoyles would frighten off evil spirits.

Building Blocks

ARCHED WINDOW

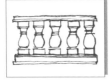

BALUSTRADE

BIFORATE WINDOW

BRACKET

GARGOYLE

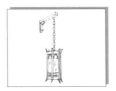

LANTERN

PEDIMENT

SPIRE

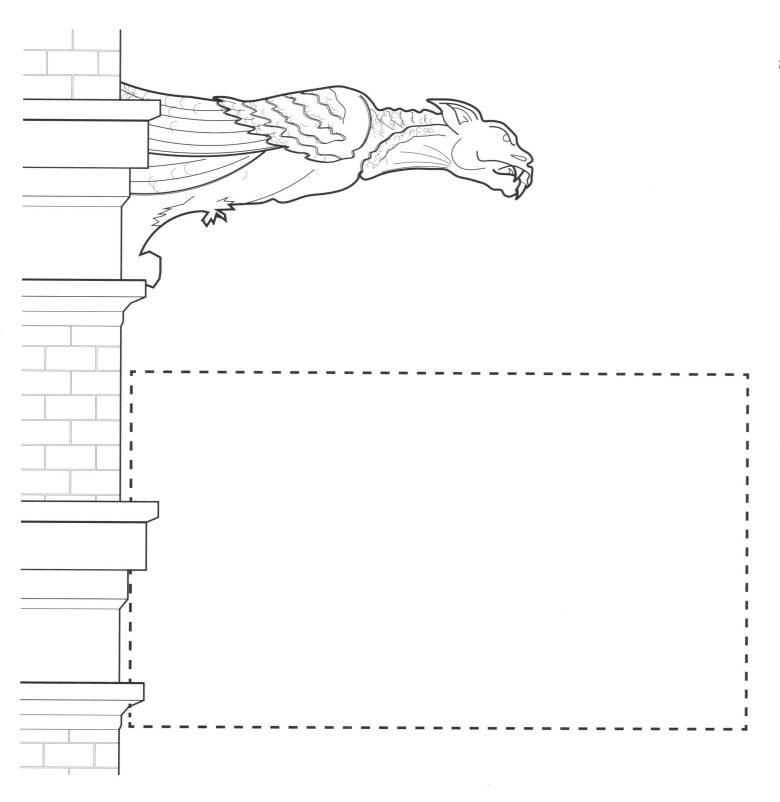

DRAW YOUR OWN GARGOYLE TO PROTECT THE BUILDING. MAKE UP YOUR OWN CREATURE!

According to legend, Gargoyles come alive at night and guard a building while the people inside are asleep.

One of the most beautiful Street Clocks in NYC is right here in front of the Sherry Netherland. Not only did they keep people on time, they also were great advertising. The clocks were a great place to meet and brought people to the storefront.

Time Check!
Before everyone had cell phones people relied on Street Clocks to tell the time. In the 1920s and 1930s, there were hundreds of these clocks in New York City. Now only seven of the original street clocks remain.

THE PLAZA HOTEL

The Plaza Hotel is one of the most famous buildings in New York City.
It was designed by the same architect as the Dakota Building on the Upper West Side walk. The Plaza resembles a French chateau. A chateau is a large French country house or castle.

When the hotel opened in 1907, this area was becoming the most exclusive neighborhood in the city. Private mansions and posh apartment buildings lined Fifth Avenue. The Plaza Hotel was built to welcome the most distinguished visitors.

Year Built
1907
Architect
Henry J. Hardenburgh
Style
French Second Empire (Baroque)
Materials
Glazed Brick, Copper roof

The Plaza is the setting for the Eloise books by Kay Thompson and illustrated by Hilary Knight. Inside, you can see the "Eloise Suite" or have an Eloise themed tea in the Palm Court.

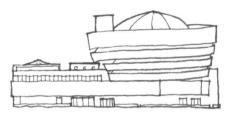

The famous architect, Frank Lloyd Wright used the Plaza Hotel as his headquarters while he was designing the Guggenheim Museum.

Building Blocks

ARCHED WINDOW

CUPOLA

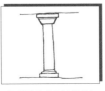

DORIC COLUMN

FRIEZE

KEY PATTERN

MANSARD ROOF

PILASTER

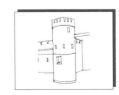

TURRET

LOOK UP! *at the fancy entrance to the Plaza. Red carpet, gold decoration, stained glass windows and colorful flags.*

The flags outside the Plaza Hotel change for different occasions in the city or if they have a special visitor. The American flag and the Plaza logo are always flown.

DESIGN THE FLAGS FOR YOUR OWN HOTEL

An old commercial for the Plaza said "Nothing Unimportant Ever Happens at The Plaza."

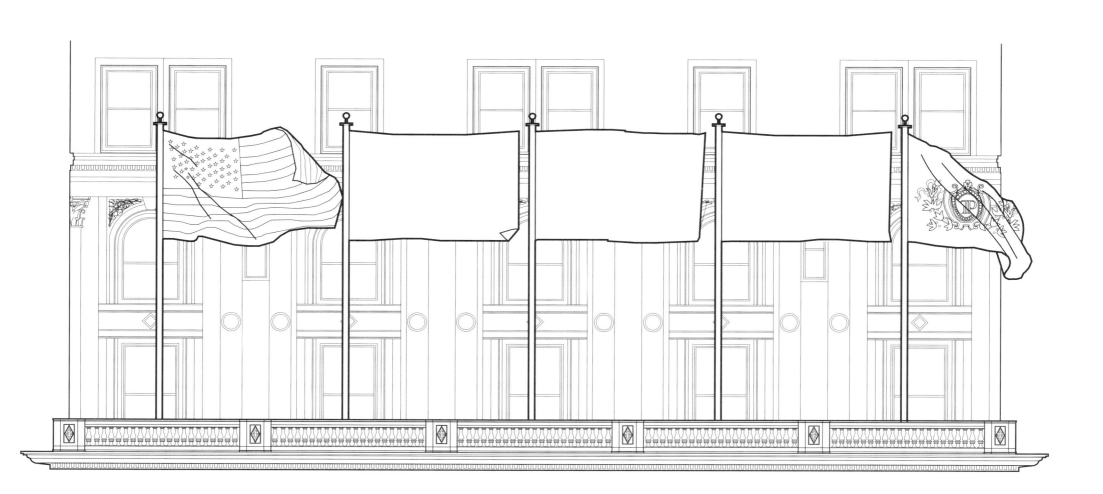

THE APPLE STORE

The Apple Store is the only example of Modern Architecture on this Upper East Side walk. Modern Architecture has very little ornamentation and draws our attention to the building materials. In this case, the building material is glass.

Year Built
2006
Architect
Bohlin Cywinski Jackson
Style
Modern
Materials
Glass

The glass cube is totally self-supporting. There is no structural steel.

The glass spiral staircase, which has its very own patent, is inside a cylinder of glass. It draws the customers down to the main floor where you can see all of the products.

The apple image you see on the Apple Store and its products is a registered trademark of Apple Inc.

Building Blocks

CANOPY

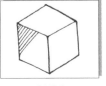

CUBE

CURTAINWALL

GLASS BEAMS

GLASS CLIPS

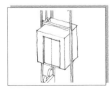

GLASS ELEVATOR

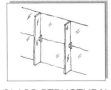

GLASS STRUCTURAL FINS

SPIRAL STAIR

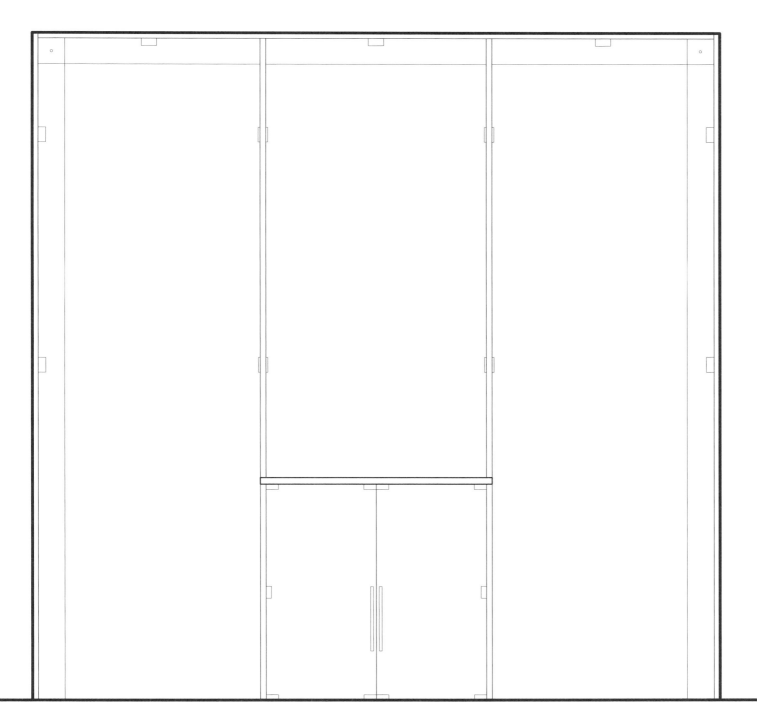

LOOK UP! *at the Apple logo floating inside the Apple Store building. A logo is a symbol or design that identifies a company or a product. It should be easy to spot and eye-catching so people remember it.*

DESIGN YOUR OWN PERSONAL LOGO FOR THE STORE

It could be your name written in an interesting way or using a certain color, a symbol that is special to you or a combination of all three!

 Placing signs around a building is often part of an Architect's design. The signs themselves are usually designed by a graphic designer. Their work is to create a signature look for a company or a product.

The Apple logo is one of the most recognizable logos of all time.
What are some of your favorite logos?

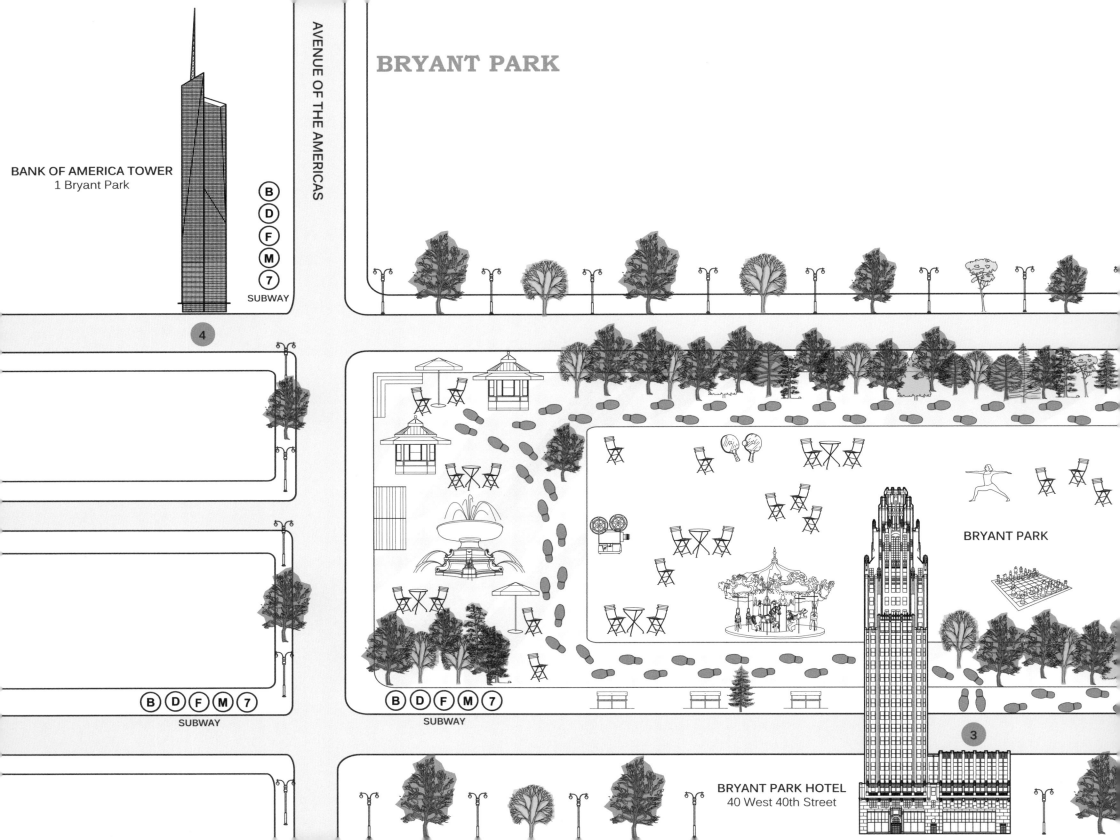

BRYANT PARK

BANK OF AMERICA TOWER
1 Bryant Park

AVENUE OF THE AMERICAS

(B)
(D)
(F)
(M)
(7)
SUBWAY

4

(B) (D) (F) (M) (7)
SUBWAY

(B) (D) (F) (M) (7)
SUBWAY

BRYANT PARK

3

BRYANT PARK HOTEL
40 West 40th Street

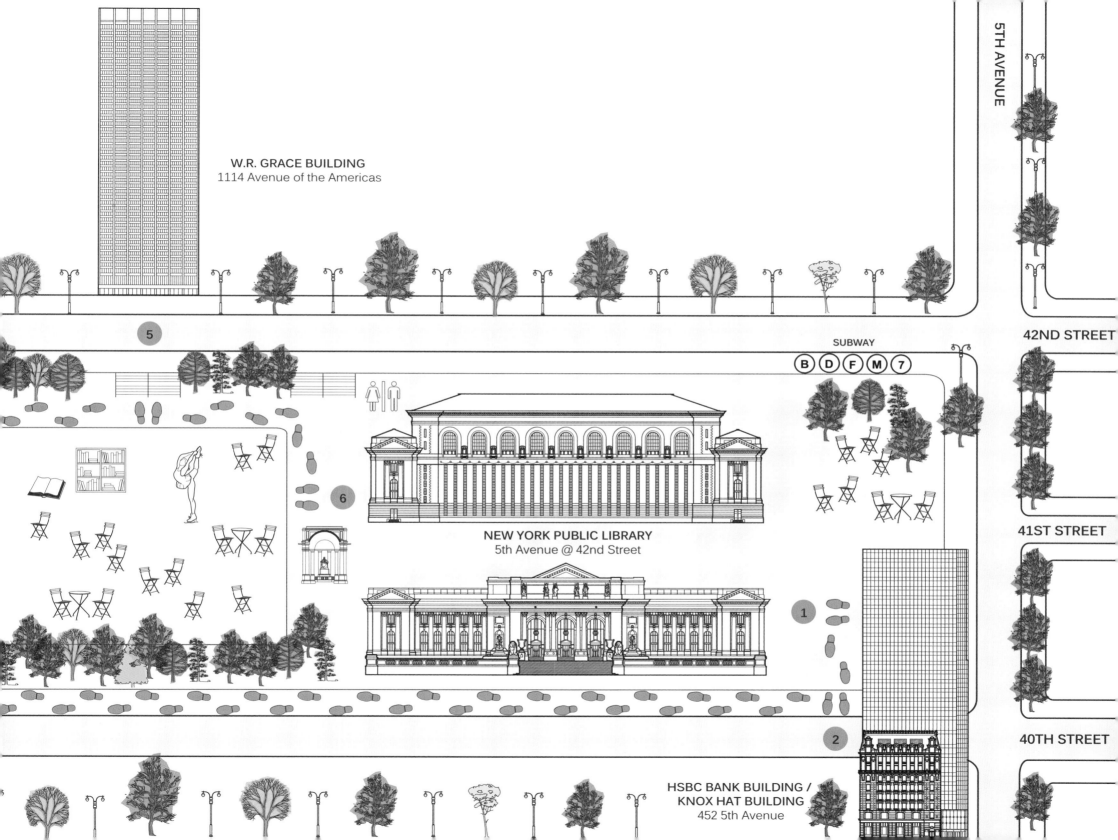

W.R. GRACE BUILDING
1114 Avenue of the Americas

5TH AVENUE

42ND STREET

5

SUBWAY

B D F M 7

41ST STREET

6

NEW YORK PUBLIC LIBRARY
5th Avenue @ 42nd Street

1

40TH STREET

2

**HSBC BANK BUILDING /
KNOX HAT BUILDING**
452 5th Avenue

THE NEW YORK PUBLIC LIBRARY
Front Facade 5th Avenue

Year Built
1898-1911
Architect
Carrere & Hastings
Style
Beaux Arts
Materials
Granite, Marble

This building has been called a "Palace for the People." The architecture of the main branch of the New York Public Library represents the real spirit of New York City. Rich or poor, all citizens should be able to enjoy beautiful public spaces.

The library has 75 miles of shelves. It took a whole year just to set up all the books.

Nearly 50,000 people visited the new library on the day it opened in 1911.

The public Reading Room is almost 300 feet long.

The library's 18 million books are stored underground beneath Bryant Park.

The Library Lions
The famous lions were sculpted by Edward Clark Potter. They were first named Leo Astor and Leo Lenox for the founders of the library, In the 1930s the mayor of New York City renamed them Patience and Fortitude.

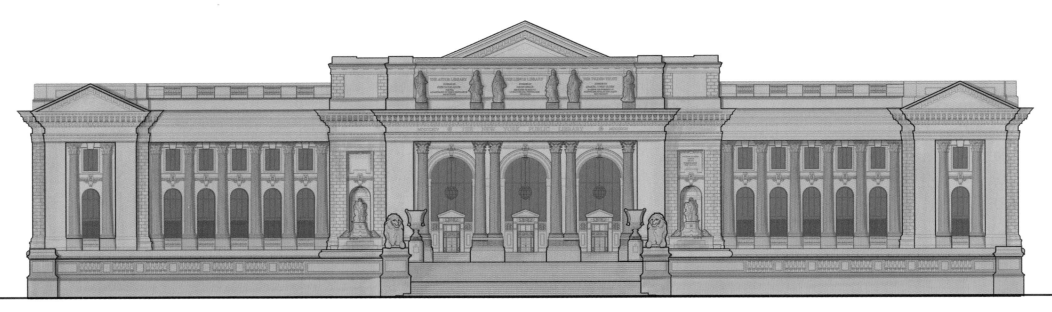

Building Blocks

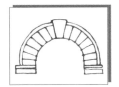

ARCH

BALUSTRADE

CORINTHIAN COLUMN

CORNICE

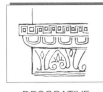

DECORATIVE FRIEZE

NICHE

PEDIMENT

SCULPTURE

DRAW A SCULPTURE OF YOURSELF INSIDE THE NICHE WELCOMING THE VISITORS TO THE LIBRARY

Brooklyn-born artist, Frederick William MacMonnies sculpted the fountains and figures in the niches of the library entrance. They are named Truth and Beauty.

The fountains in front of the library were out of commission for over 30 years. They were restored in 2015.

Ask the Architect! Marble is formed when limestone is heated and pressed in nature. The minerals change chemically and form the patterns that you see on the surface. The library's marble comes from Vermont and is three feet thick.

HSBC BANK BUILDING / KNOX HAT BUILDING

The HSBC Bank Building was built around the Knox Hat Building. The Knox Hat Building is a New York City Landmark. The architects of the modern bank wanted to preserve the historic building.

Year Built
Knox Hat 1902
Architect
John Duncan
Style
Beaux Arts
Materials
Limestone, Copper

Year Built
HSBC 1983
Architect
Attia & Perkins
Style
Post Modern
Materials
Glass, Steel

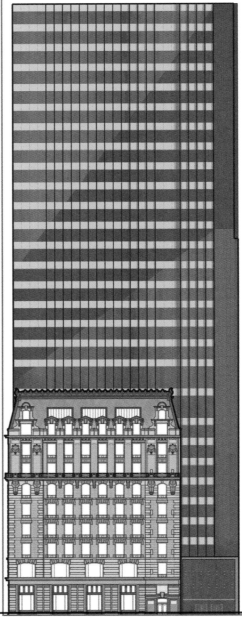

The Architects wanted the new building to create a background to compliment the older building. The tower looks like a glass curtain behind the Knox Building.

Two other buildings are built into the glass tower too! Turn the corner and look down Fifth Avenue.

The Knox Hat Building was the headquarters of the Knox Hat Company, one of the largest, most successful hat companies in New York from 1838 until the 1960s when formal hats (sadly) went out of style.

Building Blocks

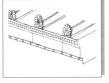
ANTEFIX

BRACKET

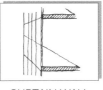
CURTAIN WALL

DORMER

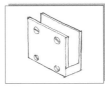
GLASS CLIP

MULLION

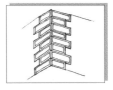
QUOINS

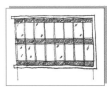
SPANDREL

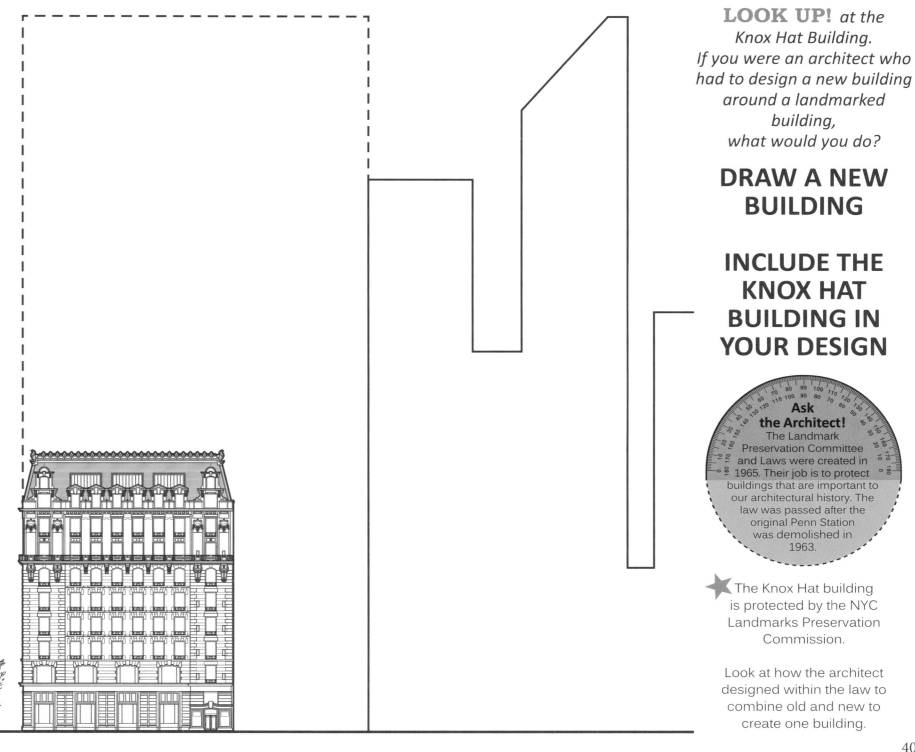

LOOK UP! *at the Knox Hat Building.*
If you were an architect who had to design a new building around a landmarked building,
what would you do?

DRAW A NEW BUILDING

INCLUDE THE KNOX HAT BUILDING IN YOUR DESIGN

Ask the Architect! The Landmark Preservation Committee and Laws were created in 1965. Their job is to protect buildings that are important to our architectural history. The law was passed after the original Penn Station was demolished in 1963.

★ The Knox Hat building is protected by the NYC Landmarks Preservation Commission.

Look at how the architect designed within the law to combine old and new to create one building.

THE BRYANT PARK HOTEL

The striking Bryant Park Hotel was originally the headquarters for the American Radiator Company and was commonly known as The American Radiator Building.

Contrasting colors really make this building stand out.

It was said that the black brick resembled coal and the gold terra cotta looked like fire. These building materials represented the radiator company perfectly. Coal and fire supply the heat for a radiator.

Year Built
1924
Architect
Hood & Fouliboux
Style
Art Deco
Materials
Brick, Terra Cotta

The architects liked the dark brick because the color didn't contrast as much with the windows. This made the building appear more solid.

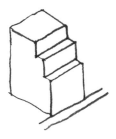

This is one of the first buildings built after the new 1916 setback Zoning laws. The law required tall buildings to be setback from the street to let in more light and fresh air.

Each setback is accented with gold terra cotta. By the time you get to the top of the tower, it is mostly gold. The architects used the setback law to strengthen their design and draw your eye to the gold decoration.

The Radiator Building was the first New York City skyscraper with powerful outdoor lighting. The upper floors glowed with light at night. The sight inspired artist, Georgia O'Keefe to paint *Radiator Building-Night* in 1927.

Building Blocks

ARCHED WINDOW

BRACKET

DECORATIVE FRIEZE

DENTIL MOULDING

ENTRY

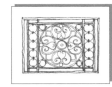
IRONWORK GUARDRAIL

LANTERN

TOWER

WHAT CAN YOU SEE BEHIND THE GLASS?
USE YOUR IMAGINATION!

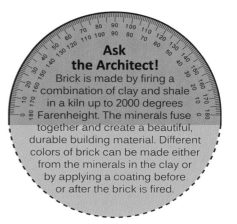

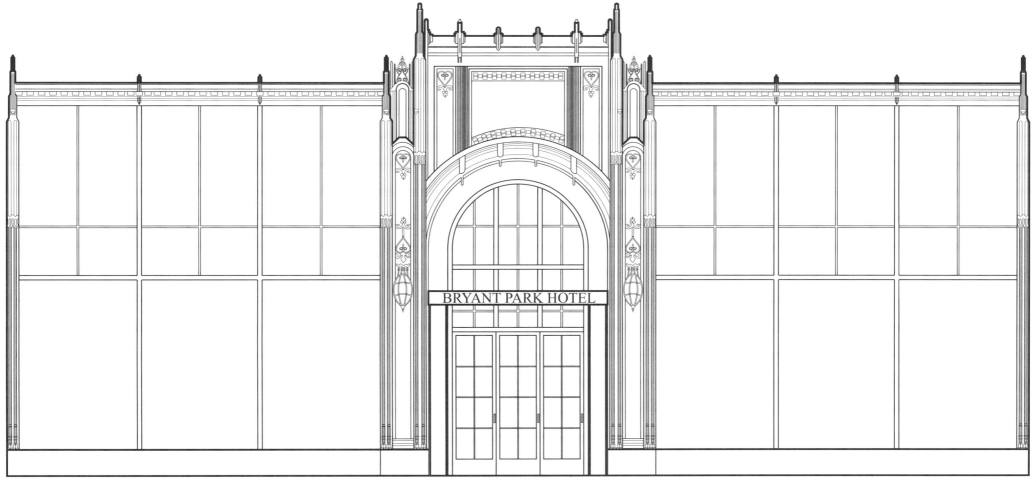

BRYANT PARK HOTEL

BANK OF AMERICA

The Bank of America Tower is a very special skyscraper. Not only is it one of the tallest buildings in New York City, it is also the very first skyscraper to receive the highest honor for "Green'" building.

The building was awarded LEED (Leadership in Energy and Efficient Design) Platinum certification from the US Green Building Council.

Year Built
2009
Architect
Cook & Fox
Style
Post Modern
Materials
Steel and Glass

What is GREEN building?

It means the building is designed in ways that are better for our environment. It uses recycled materials and finds ways to reduce its use of resources. Another name for building Green is Sustainable Design.

It also means that the building is healthier for the people who work there. Lots of windows for light and fresh air, beautiful public areas for breaks, and views of the park.

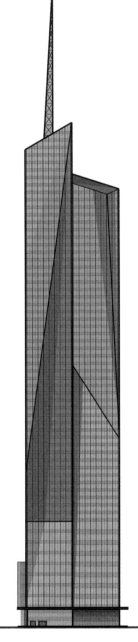

Some of the ways this building is **GREEN**

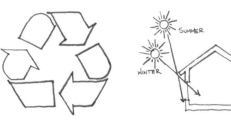

★ **Uses recycled and recyclable materials**

★ **Air entering the building is filtered**

★ **Uses Daylighting strategies which saves energy by relying on the sun to light the space**

★ **Glazing on windows contain heat reducing glass but still maximizes light**

★ **Grey water system reuses rainwater**

★ **Green Roof areas release oxygen into the air and give people a view of nature**

Building Blocks

ARCHITECTURAL SPIRE

CANOPY

CONCRETE COLUMN

CURTAIN WALL

METAL FIN

MULLION

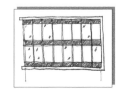
SPANDREL

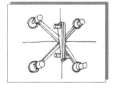
SPIDER CONNECTION

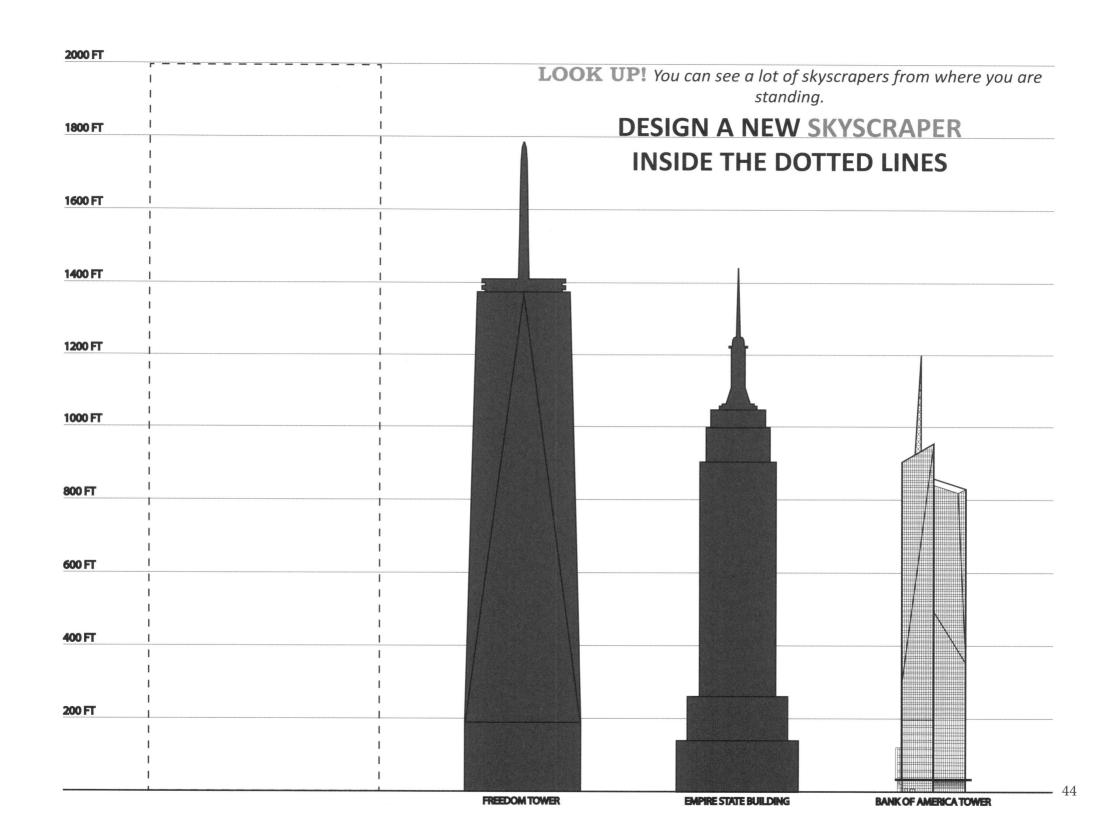

LOOK UP! *You can see a lot of skyscrapers from where you are standing.*

DESIGN A NEW SKYSCRAPER
INSIDE THE DOTTED LINES

2000 FT
1800 FT
1600 FT
1400 FT
1200 FT
1000 FT
800 FT
600 FT
400 FT
200 FT

FREEDOM TOWER

EMPIRE STATE BUILDING

BANK OF AMERICA TOWER

44

THE W.R. GRACE BUILDING

The W.R. Grace Building meets the setback requirements in a very creative way. Can you see how?

The whole building slopes up as it gets higher so the higher floors are further back from the street.

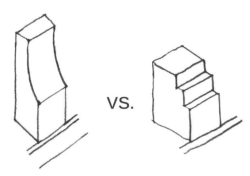

VS.

Year Built
1974
Architect
Skidmore, Owings & Merrill
Style
Modern
Materials
Travertine

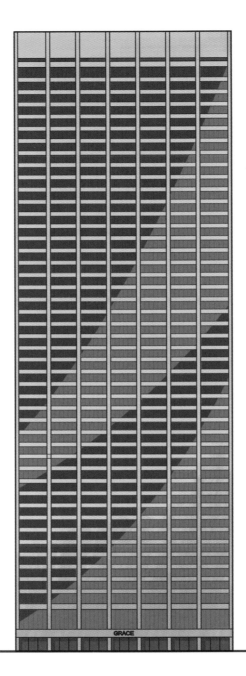

Sneak Peek!
While standing on the corner of Fifth Avenue and 42nd Street, take a look East down 42nd Street for a great view of the famous **Chrysler Building**.

Unlike the other Modern buildings you have seen, this one is made of travertine. Travertine is similar to limestone but it is created from mineral deposits. The deposits make it rougher and more porous instead of smooth like limestone. It was one of the first building stones used by the Roman Empire.

The white travertine contrasts with the dark windows. This contrast makes the building appear lighter than the other buildings. The effect is the exact opposite of the contrast between the windows and black brick of the Bryant Park Hotel.

The largest building in the world constructed from Travertine is the Roman Colloseum.

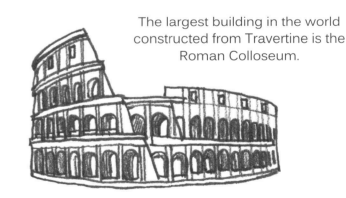

Building Blocks

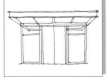

CANOPY

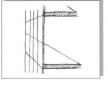

CURTAIN WALL

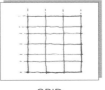

GRID

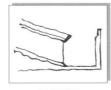

GUTTER

MULLION

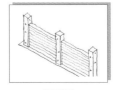

PIERS

PLAZA

REVOLVING DOOR

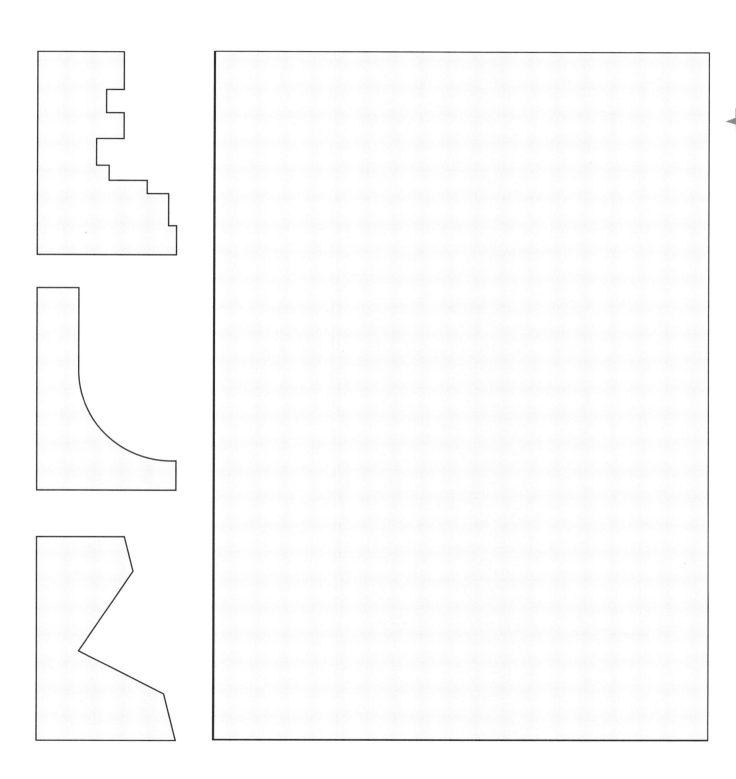

LOOK UP! *at the W.R Grace Building.*

When you look at the WR Grace Building **elevation** *(front view), it looks like an average rectangular building.*

Kind of boring....

But when you look at it from the side, you can see what makes it special. It swoops down like a giant slide!

LOOK AT THE INTERESTING SIDE VIEW ELEVATIONS DRAWN HERE

WHICH ONE IS THE WR GRACE BUILDING?

DESIGN A FUN SIDE ELEVATION FOR YOUR VERY OWN BUILDING

THE NEW YORK PUBLIC LIBRARY
Rear Facade Bryant Park

Year Built
1898-1911
Architect
Carrere & Hastings
Style
Beaux Arts
Materials
Granite, Marble

The back of the library building faces a public plaza, Bryant Park. It was designed just as thoughtfully as the front entrance.

The idea of designing a building on all sides was new. Lots of buildings had a beautiful entrance but the back of the building, which wasn't seen from the street, was very plain.

The library was built on the site of the Croton Resevoir which was demolished in 1899. The resevoir held water reserves and was enclosed by a high stone wall. People could walk around the walkway on top of the wall for great views of the city.

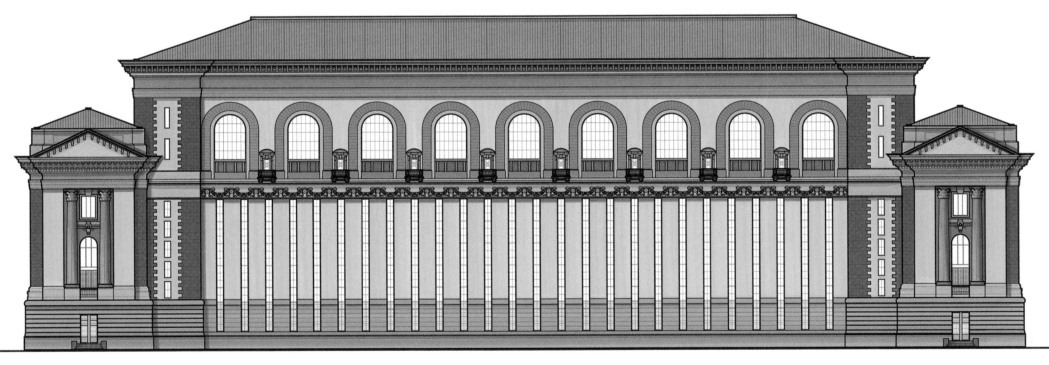

Building Blocks

ARCHED WINDOW

BALCONY

BALUSTRADE

DECORATIVE FRIEZE

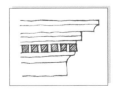
DENTIL MOULDING

PILASTER

QUOINS

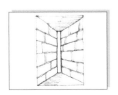
SLOTTED WINDOW

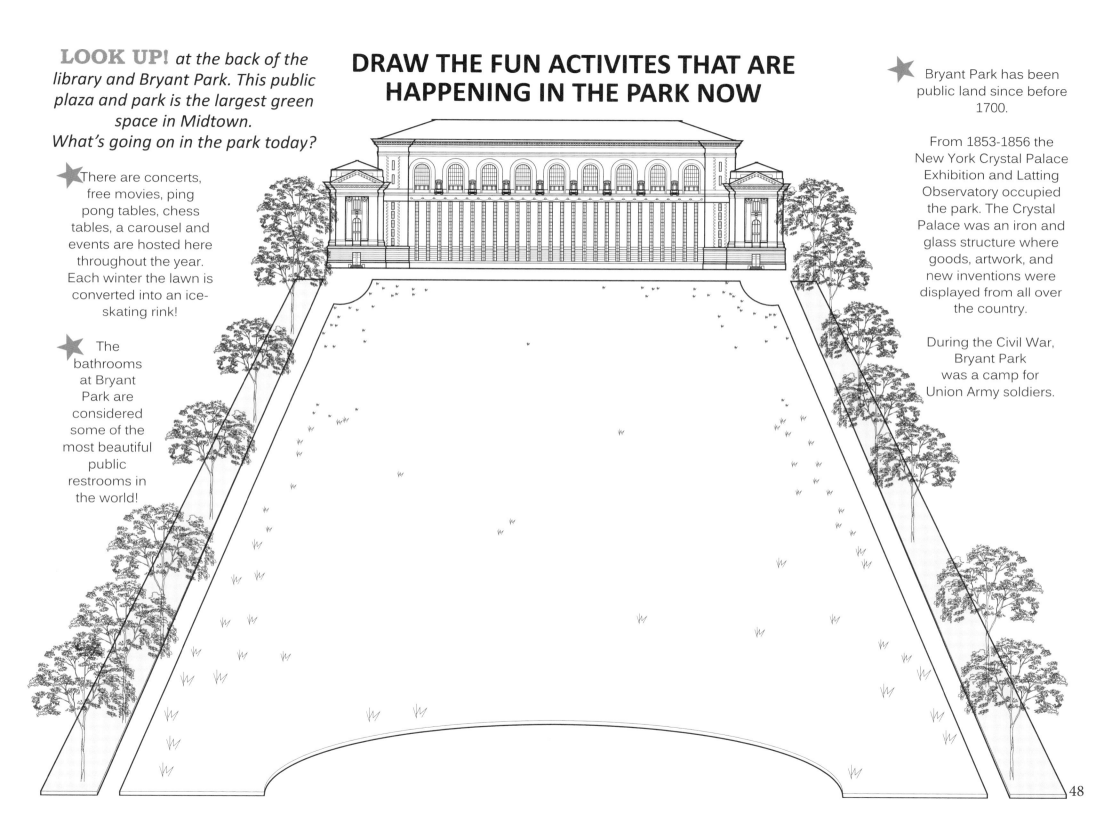

LOOK UP! *at the back of the library and Bryant Park. This public plaza and park is the largest green space in Midtown.*
What's going on in the park today?

★ There are concerts, free movies, ping pong tables, chess tables, a carousel and events are hosted here throughout the year. Each winter the lawn is converted into an ice-skating rink!

★ The bathrooms at Bryant Park are considered some of the most beautiful public restrooms in the world!

DRAW THE FUN ACTIVITES THAT ARE HAPPENING IN THE PARK NOW

★ Bryant Park has been public land since before 1700.

From 1853-1856 the New York Crystal Palace Exhibition and Latting Observatory occupied the park. The Crystal Palace was an iron and glass structure where goods, artwork, and new inventions were displayed from all over the country.

During the Civil War, Bryant Park was a camp for Union Army soldiers.

48

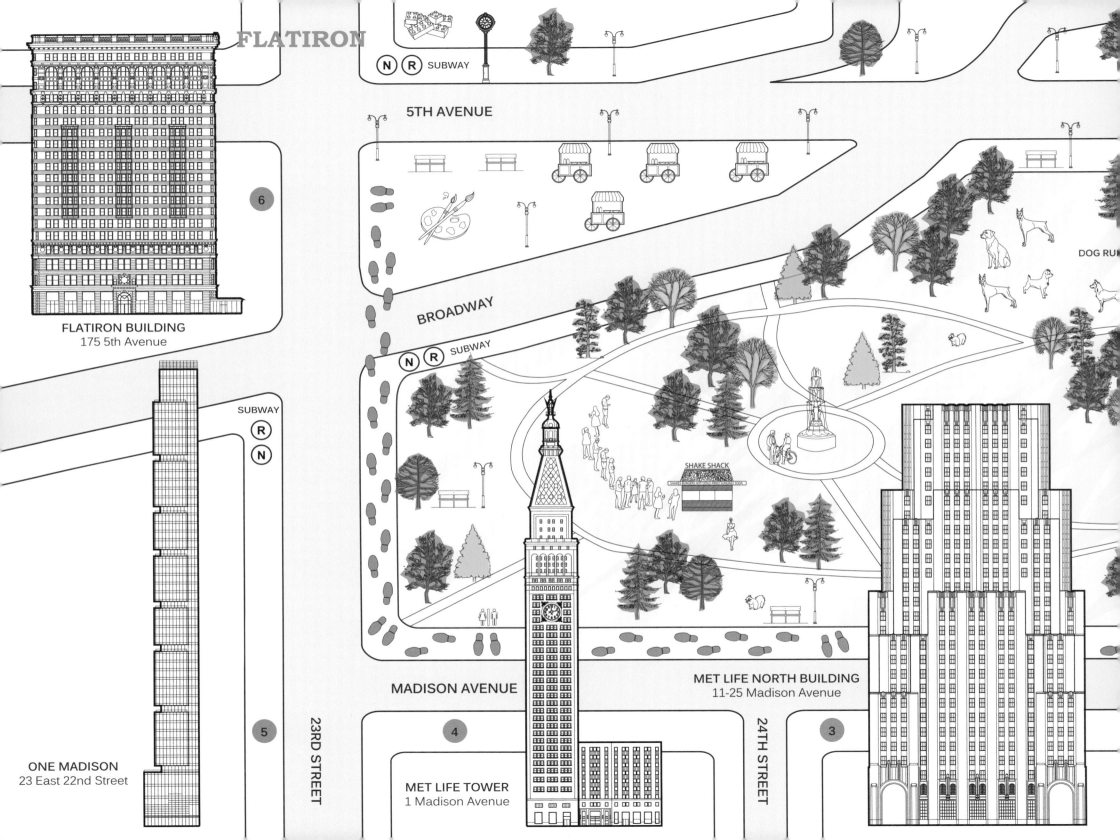

FLATIRON

FLATIRON BUILDING
175 5th Avenue

6

ONE MADISON
23 East 22nd Street

5

SUBWAY
R
N

23RD STREET

5TH AVENUE

BROADWAY

N R SUBWAY

N R SUBWAY

SHAKE SHACK
SHAKES BURGERS HOT DOGS FRIED SUNDAES SODA

DOG RU

MADISON AVENUE

MET LIFE NORTH BUILDING
11-25 Madison Avenue

24TH STREET

4

3

MET LIFE TOWER
1 Madison Avenue

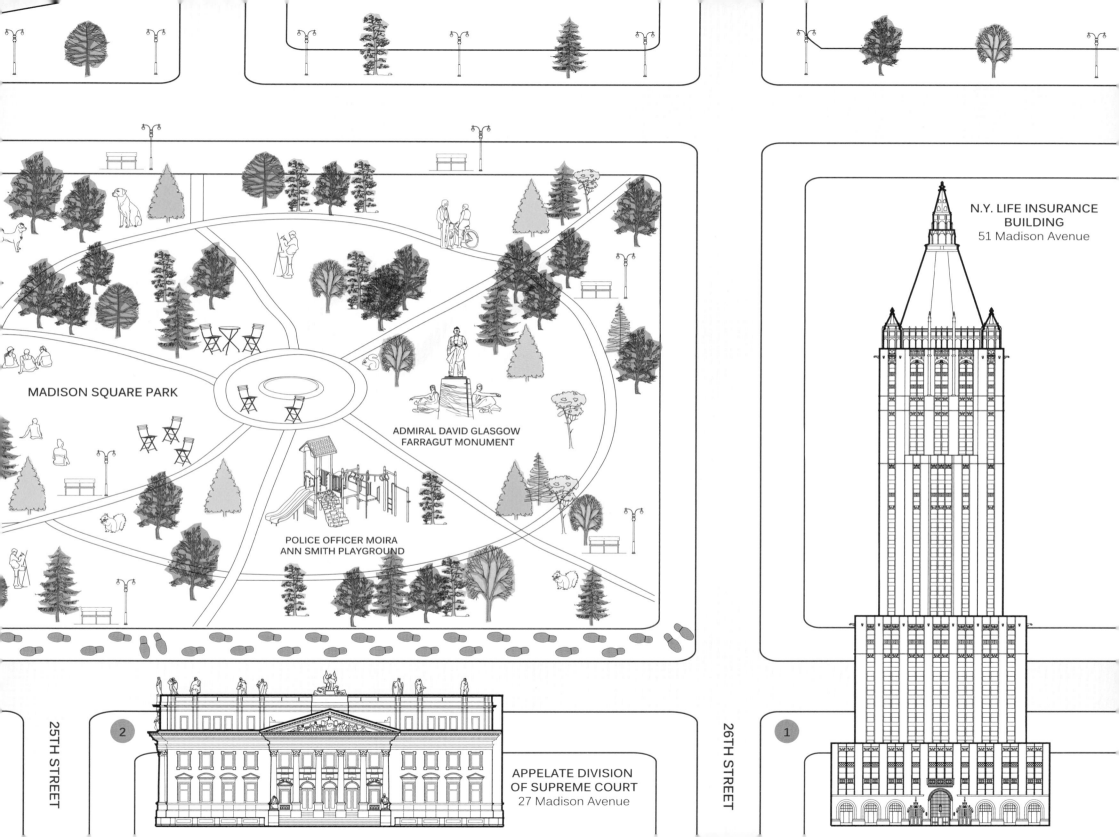

MADISON SQUARE PARK

ADMIRAL DAVID GLASGOW
FARRAGUT MONUMENT

POLICE OFFICER MOIRA
ANN SMITH PLAYGROUND

N.Y. LIFE INSURANCE
BUILDING
51 Madison Avenue

APPELATE DIVISION
OF SUPREME COURT
27 Madison Avenue

25TH STREET

26TH STREET

2

1

NEW YORK LIFE INSURANCE BUILDING

The headquarters for the New York Life Insurance Company is 40 stories in all, including the six story gold pyramid. Near the top you can see some of the Gothic elements like gargoyles and tracery that give the building its style.

The building has a huge base. It covers an entire city block. It is topped by a tower with a gold crown which is lit up at night.

Year Built
1928
Architect
Cass Gilbert
Style
Neo-Gothic
Materials
Limestone

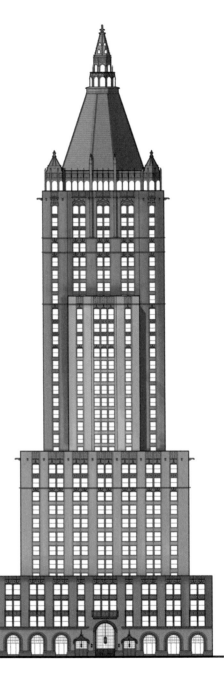

The tower roof was originally covered in gold-leaf.
It has since been replaced with gold colored tiles.

This building site has seen it all! As a railroad depot, a concert hall, then PT Barnum's Hippodrome, where he presented the early versions of his circus show. Until 1925, the original Madison Square Garden stood here, designed by the notable architect, Stanford White, who was murdered in the roof garden theatre of his own building in 1906.

Building Blocks

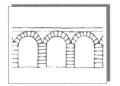

ARCADE

BALCONY

BIFORATE WINDOW

GARGOYLE

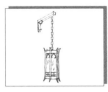

LANTERN

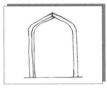

POINTED ARCH

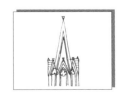

SPIRE

TRACERY

CONNECT THE DOTS AND SEE WHAT YOU FIND

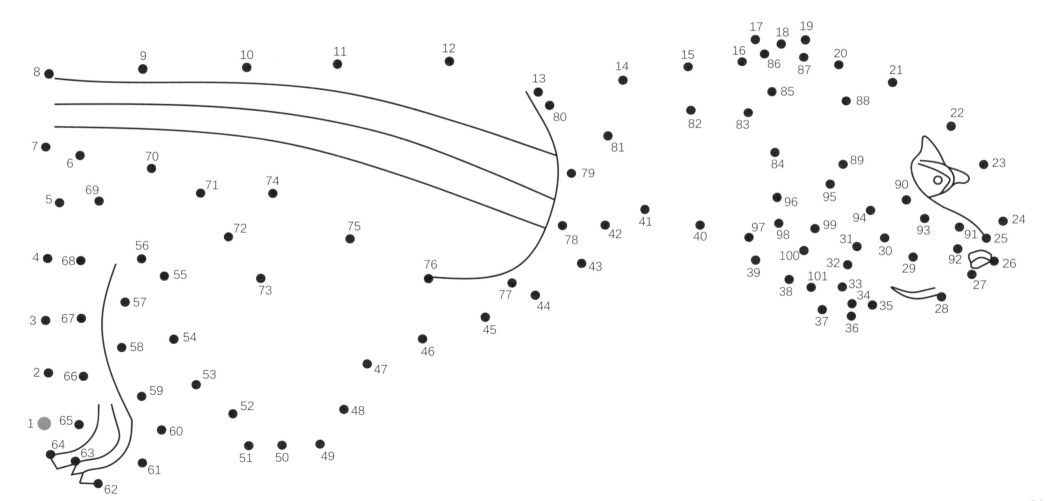

APPELLATE DIVISION OF THE SUPREME COURT FOR THE STATE OF NEW YORK

Year Built
1900
Architect
James Brown Lord
Style
Beaux Arts
Materials
Limestone

Although quite small compared to the giant buildings that surround it, the Appellate Division Courthouse makes up for its small size with its beautiful design.

The building is one of the best examples of **The City Beautiful Movement of the 1890s creating monumental architecture in U.S. cities**. The architects and city planners that were involved felt that making beautiful buildings, plazas and parks for people to enjoy would create a city of splendor and harmony.

The oversized pediment, huge Corinthian columns and the large variety of sculpture are what give the courthouse its character. Sixteen of the most famous sculptors of the time contributed work, including Edward James Potter who also sculpted the Library Lions.

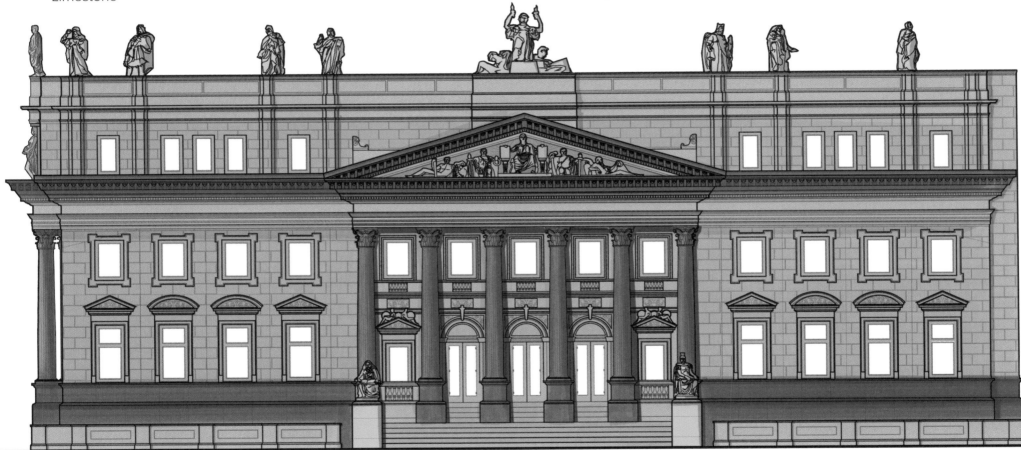

Building Blocks

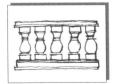

BALUSTRADE

CORINTHIAN COLUMN

CORNICE

FRIEZE

DECORATIVE FRIEZE

PEDIMENT

PILASTER

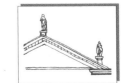

SCULPTURE

LOOK UP! *at the Appellate Division Courthouse Building.*
The sculpture on the roof and inside the pediment tells this building's story.
What story would you like to tell?

DRAW YOUR OWN STORY INSIDE THE PEDIMENT

The most famous sculptural pediments were part of the Parthenon in Ancient Greece. One told the story of the Greek goddess Athena being born from her father Zeus's head. Another illustrated a famous battle between Athena and the sea god, Poseidon, for control over the city of Athens.

Ask the Architect!
Architectural sculpture is incorporated into the building design. The sculpted elements are meant to decorate and enhance the look of the building. The sculpture also supports the buildings' purpose. On this courthouse, the sculptures relate to the subject of law.

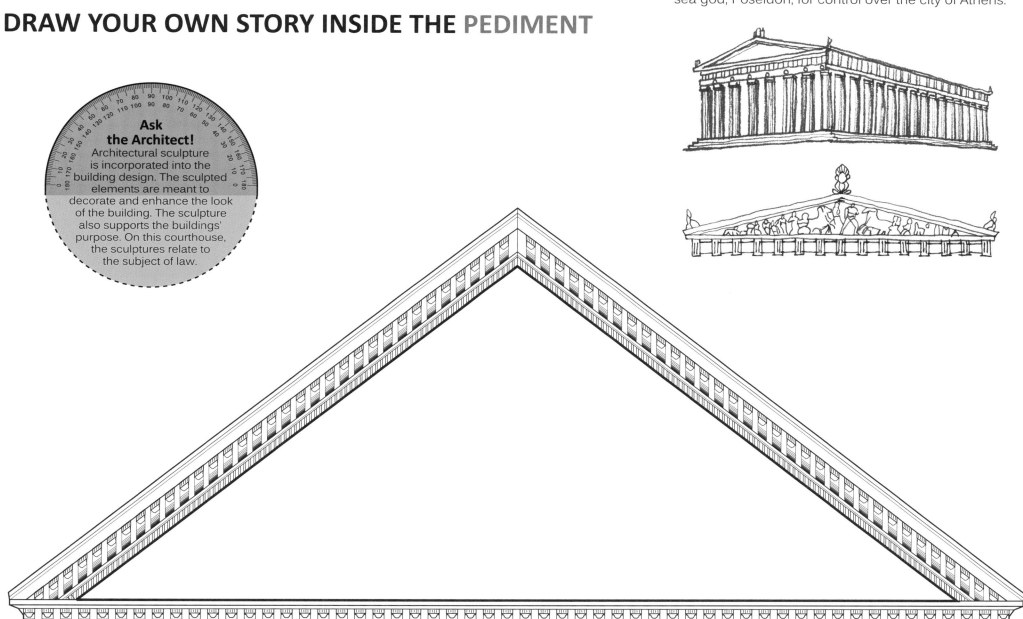

METROPOLITAN LIFE NORTH BUILDING

The North Building of the Metropolitan Life Insurance Company was originally designed to be a 100-story skyscraper. Construction was stopped after the 29th floor because of the Great Depression.

What you see here is only the base of the original design.

Doesn't it look like it's missing something?

Year Built
1932
Architect
Harvey Wiley Corbett and D. Everett Waid
Style
Art Deco
Materials
Limestone, Marble

The shape that a building makes on the ground is called the building's **footprint.** This building's footprint is a full city block.

A big **footprint** usually means a very tall building. Most tall skyscrapers have a larger base and get narrower as they go up.

The footprint of this building is so big because it was designed to be the base of a 100-story tower. The arcade entrances on each corner also look outsized. They are the right proportion for a skyscraper, not a 29-story building.

Here is a sketch of what the building was intended to look like.

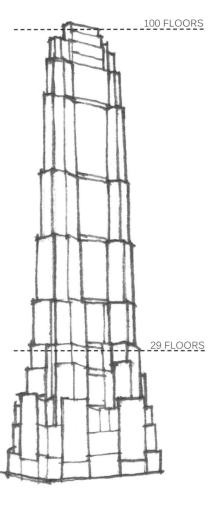

100 FLOORS

29 FLOORS

Building Blocks

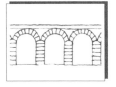

ARCADE

ARCHED WINDOW

PILASTER

SASH WINDOW

SCULPTED GRILLE

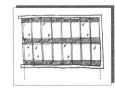

SPANDREL

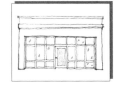

STOREFRONT

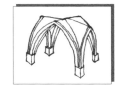

VAULTED CEILING

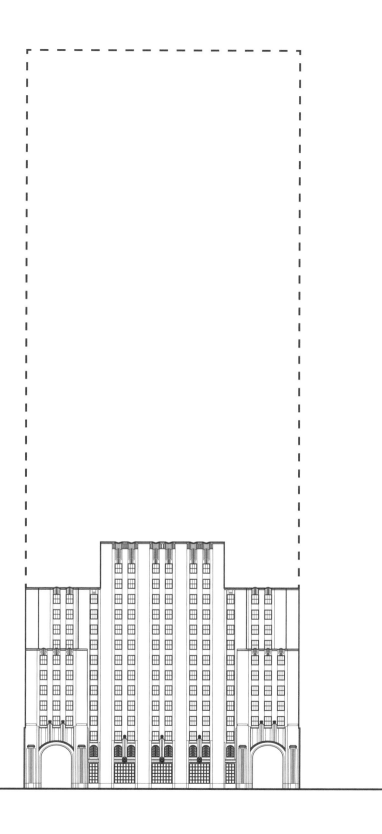

LOOK UP! *at the North Building of the Met Life Insurance Company.*

This building was intended to be a 100-story tower but construction was stopped during the Great Depression.

How would you design this building to make it the skyscraper it was supposed to be?

FINISH THE SKYSCRAPER
DESIGN A NEW TOWER

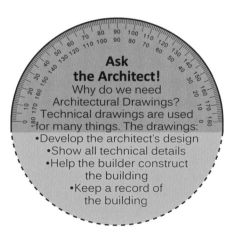

Ask the Architect!
Why do we need Architectural Drawings? Technical drawings are used for many things. The drawings:
• Develop the architect's design
• Show all technical details
• Help the builder construct the building
• Keep a record of the building

MET LIFE TOWER

The Met Life Tower was added to the 1893, 11-story Met Life East wing in 1909. With 51 stories, it was the tallest building in the world for four years. The Woolworth Building took that title in 1913.

The tower was renovated in the early 1960s and most of its original ornamentation was removed. The building's marble facade was covered with limestone to give it a more modern look.

Year Built
1909
Architect
Napoleon Le Brun and Sons
Style
Art Deco
Materials
Limestone

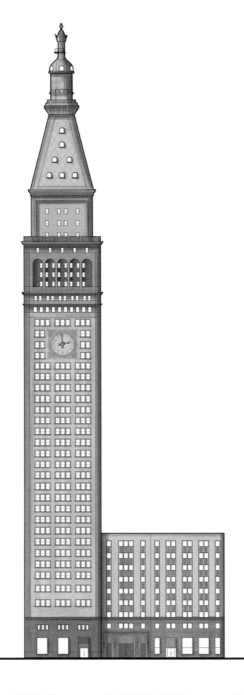

The gold cupola at the top of the tower lights up at night. Just like the Empire State Building, it changes color for different holidays and other big events.

Each number on the clockface is 4 feet tall.

Building Blocks

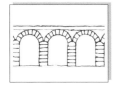
ARCADE

ARCHED WINDOW

BALCONY

BALUSTRADE

DOME

DORMER WINDOW

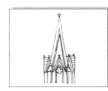
SPIRE

TRIPARTE WINDOW

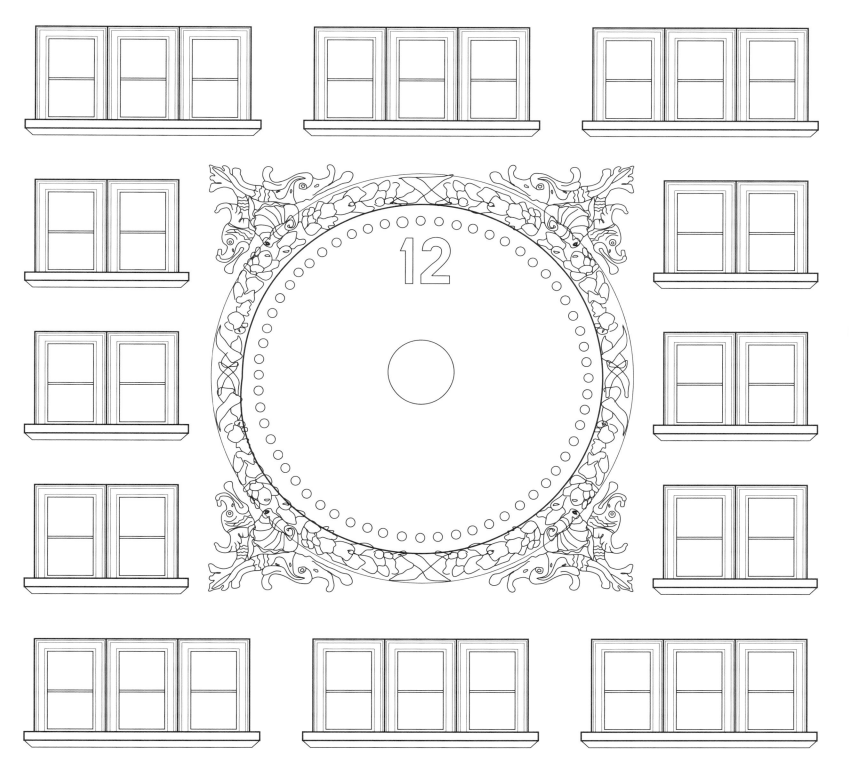

WHAT IS YOUR FAVORITE TIME OF DAY?

DRAW THE CLOCKFACE WITH YOUR FAVORITE TIME

★ The four clocks, one on each side of the building survived the 1960's renovation although they were rebuilt. Each clock is three stories high.

ONE MADISON PARK

One Madison Park is one of the only modern buildings facing Madison Square Park. It is an interesting contrast to all the historical buildings around it.

The building is 60 stories tall. Its slender design and glass facade make it seem delicate compared to the massive limestone and marble buildings you have seen on this walk so far.

Year Built
2009
Architect
Cetra/Ruddy Architects
Style
Post Modern
Materials
Glass, Concrete

Although the base of One Madison looks very small from where you stand, it actually extends back from the street entrance to the other block!

Living in a glass box? The 360 degree views must be amazing. But if you can see out, can everyone else see in?

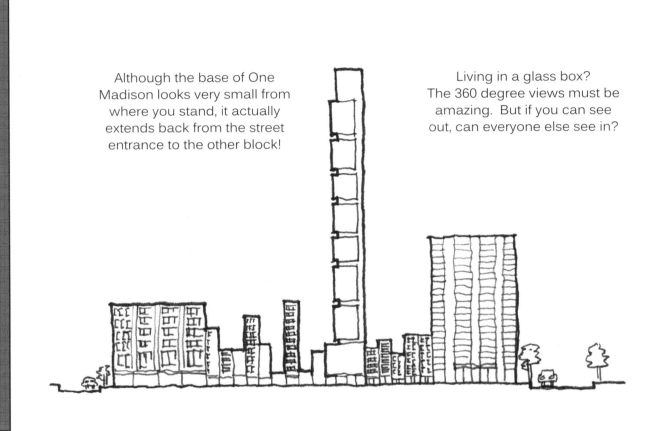

Building Blocks

BALCONY

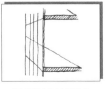

CURTAIN WALL

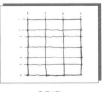

GRID

MULLION

NICHE

REVOLVING DOOR

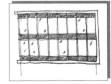

SPANDREL

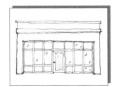

STOREFRONT

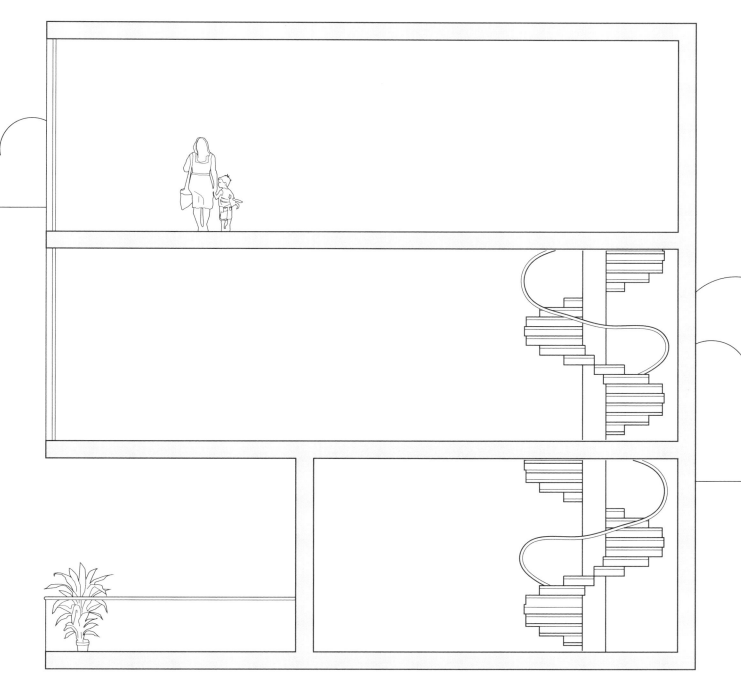

LOOK UP! *at*
One Madison Park

This building looks like a stack of glass boxes.

How would you like to live in a glass box in the sky?

DRAW YOUR DREAM HOUSE IN THE CLOUDS

Ask the Architect!
Like steel, glass can be used structurally. It is made by heating clear sand, calcium oxide and sodium carbonite at high temperatures and then cooled. The cooling process determines the strength of the glass. Other materials can be added to increase the strength or give it qualities like color or energy efficiancy.

FLATIRON BUILDING

The Flatiron Building is best known for its unique triangular shape. Remember that the shape that a building makes on the ground is called the building's **footprint.**
The Flatiron's footprint is in the shape of a triangle because of the way Broadway crosses Fifth Avenue at the point where the building stands.
The building's triangular shape fills the entire site.

People were afraid the strange shape would make the building unstable. However, the architect used a steel structure. The steel skeleton gives the building strength and flexibility.

Year Built
1902
Architect
Daniel H. Burnham
Style
Beaux Arts
Materials
Limestone, Terra Cotta

Another name for footprint is **plan**. Architects use plans in different ways. A plan is a horizontal slice of the building. It shows the space the building will occupy on the ground. Each floor has its own plan. A **floor plan** is like a map of the different areas on each floor.

Fifth Avenue

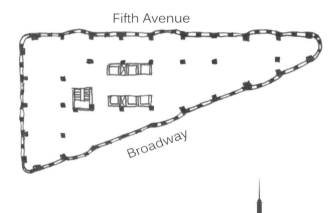

Broadway

Sneak Peek!
After looking at the Flatiron Building, turn and head north up Fifth Ave before crossing into the park, you get a great view of the **Empire State Building!**

Building Blocks

ARCHED WINDOW

BANDED COLUMN

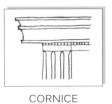

CORNICE

KEY PATTERN

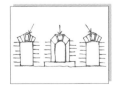

KEYSTONE

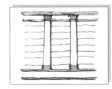

PILASTER

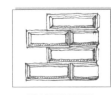

RUSTICATED STONE

STOREFRONT

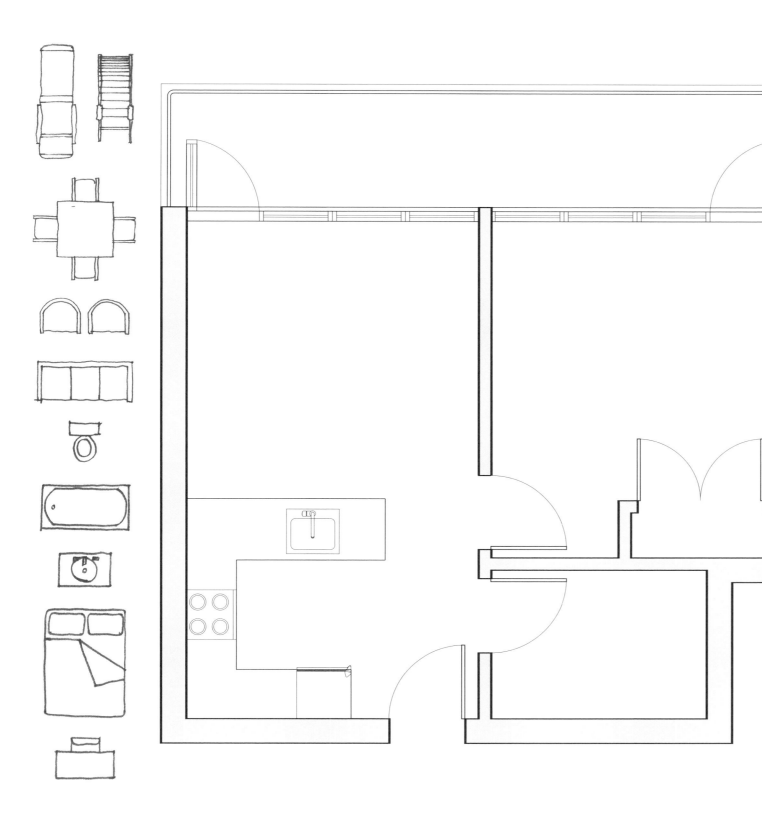

DESIGN YOUR OWN
FLOOR PLAN

YOU CAN USE THE FURNITURE SYMBOLS FOR INSPIRATION

The Flatiron is one of the most photgraphed, painted, and sketched buildings in the world.

Professional artists and amatuers alike love recreating its distinct shape.

Time Check!
Another one of the seven original street clocks sits on Fifth Avenue and 23rd Street right in front of the Lego Store. The Fifth Avenue Hotel used to occupy that building. The FAB on the clockface stands for Fifth Avenue Building.

LOOK UP! GLOSSARY of TERMS

ANTEFIX
A carved ornament that sticks up at the end of a row of roof tiles to hide the joint where the tiles meet the roof.

BALUSTRADE
A railing made of short pillars at a balcony or a window.

BUTTRESS
A large stone support built against the side of a building that keeps the walls from falling.

ARCADE
A row of arches usually creating an entrance to a building.

BATTLEMENT
The parapet or top of the building wall with regularly spaced square openings. Designed so guards could shoot at their enemy and hide from gunfire and arrows.

CABLE SYSTEM
Part of a glass wall system. The cables support the long trusses that run along the exterior glass walls.

ARCH
A semi-circle usually made of stone or brick that is set over a window or an entrance to a building.

BAY WINDOW
A curved, three-dimensional window that comes out from the building wall.

CANOPY
An overhang or covering that projects over the entrance of a building.

ARCHED WINDOW
A window opening with a semi-circular shaped top.

BIFORATE WINDOW
A window divided down the center with two openings, usually arched and common in Medieval architecture.

CARTOUCHE
An oval decorative panel that might have different carvings or inscriptions.

ARCHITECTURAL SPIRE
A tall skinny structure built on a roof that ends with a point.

BRACKET
A carved piece of stone jutting from a building wall that supports another building part.

CHIMNEY
A part of a fireplace that carries the smoke out of a building.

BALCONY
A platform that sticks out of a building surrounded by a railing or balustrade accessed by an upper-story window or door.

BROKEN ARCH
An arch that is broken in the middle on the top or bottom.

CONCRETE COLUMN
A structural support made from crushed stone and cement. Typically a rectangular shape.

CONICAL ROOF
A cone-shaped roof. They are usually found on top of a narrow tower.

DENTIL MOULDING
A small square row of blocks that look like teeth. It is a decorative molding strip below a cornice.

FRIEZE
A band or strip of molding under the cornice of a building.

CORINTHIAN COLUMN
A column is a tall, round support for part of a building, usually the roof or an arch. Corinthian columns are decorated on top with leaves and flowers or fruits.

DORIC COLUMN
A column is a tall, round support for part of a building, usually for the roof or an arched opening. This type of column is fluted with a simple top and base.

FRIEZE (Decorative)
A wide band or strip of molding that has carved pictures or decoration.

CORNICE
A ledge that sticks out from the building just below the roof. The cornice is for decoration and it protects the buildings outer walls.

DORMER WINDOW
A vertical window on top of a sloped roof.

GARGOYLE
An exaggerated carved figure of an animal or human-like form projecting from the side of a building. Can be used as a spout to drain rainwater from the roof.

CUBE
A three-dimensional square.

EGG & DART MOULDING
A decorative moulding strip that forms a pattern of alternating eggs and darts.

GLASS BEAMS
Support beams for a structure made of very thick glass.

CUPOLA
A small, decorative dome on top of a turret or steeple.

ENTRANCE
A decorated entrance to a building.

GLASS CLIPS
Clips made of steel used to connect glass panels or beams.

CURTAIN WALL
Walls that enclose a building but do not support the roof. They are often made of glass.

ENTRY DOORS
Doors to enter the interior of a building.

GLASS ELEVATOR
An elevator where the car is made from sturdy glass allowing passengers to see out as they travel up or down.

GLASS FINS
Tall, structural glass panels or fins that support a glass wall in place of steel supports.

KEY PATTERN
A square maze-like line pattern used as a decorative band usually at a frieze.

NICHE
A nook set into a wall typically for a sculpture.

GRID
A pattern of straight lines often used on the exterior of glass wall buildings.

KEYSTONE
The large wedge-shaped stone in the middle of an arch. It is the last stone set in place to secure the arch.

OCULUS
A circular window often put in under the point of a pitched roof.

GUTTER
A long narrow trough that carries water off of a building.

LANCETS
Tall windows with pointed arches.

PALLADIAN WINDOW
A window with an arched section in the middle and two narrow rectangular sections on either side orignally designed by the famous architect, Palladio.

HIP ROOF
A roof that slopes down to the walls on four sides.

LANTERN
A lamp with a glass case around the light that has a handle that can be carried or hung.

PEDIMENT
A sculptural or decorative triangle over an opening in a building. Typically supported by columns.

IONIC COLUMN
A column is a tall, round support for part of a building, usually the roof or an arch. An Ionic column has a scroll shaped top that is set on a base.

METAL FINS
A long flat metal structure on the face of a building.

PIERS
A pillar or post that supports the building above.

IRONWORK GUARDRAIL
A strong fence or rail made of iron that keeps people from falling off of a balcony or floor edge.

MULLION
A vertical or horizontal element in a window that holds panes of glass.

PILASTER
A shallow pier attached to the face of a building. It is only for decoration but meant to look like a column.

PITCHED ROOF
The most common roof where two sides slope meeting at a central ridge and form a triangle.

RUSTICATED STONE
A textured, rough stone block used for building walls.

SPIDER CONNECTION
A structural corner support for a glass wall where four pieces of glass come together.

PLAZA
A public square or open space typically surrounded by buildings.

SASH WINDOW
A window with two panels of glass panes that open by moving either panel up or down.

SPIRAL STAIR
A staircase where the stairs wind around a central point in a spiral shape.

POINTED ARCH
An arch that meets at a central point.

ARCHITECTURAL GRILLE
A grate usually made of metal that creates a barrier but still allows air through. Some grilles are sculpted from other materials and more decorative.

SPIRE
A tall skinny, pyramid-like structure at the top of a tower.

QUATREFOIL
A decoration that is made with four overlapping circles.

SCULPTURE
A free-standing, three dimensional carved piece of art typically made of stone.

SWAG
A carved decoration that usually looks like draped cloth or chains of flowers or fruit.

QUOINS
Large stacked stone on the corners of a building. Usually bigger and more decorative than the building bricks.

SLOTTED WINDOW
A very narrow window that widens on the inside to allow soldiers to fire arrows while they stay covered and protected.

TOWER
A tall slender structure. It can be free-standing or part of a building. Often used in castles and churches.

REVOLVING DOOR
Three or four doors rotating around a center shaft in a circle. Typically made of glass and in a glass enclosure.

SPANDREL
A structural element of a glass curtain wall. A spandrel is usually used to hide the concrete floor behind the glass.

TRACERY
A decorative and interlacing pattern used in Gothic windows.

TRIPARTE WINDOW
A three part window. Three windows are combined with the same height to form one set.

TRUSS
A triangular structural frame for a roof and wall.

TURRET
A tower usually at the corner of a building that extends higher than the wall it is connecting. Often used in fortresses or castles.

VAULTED CEILING
A ceiling formed with arches.

WINDOW HEADER
A carved structural piece above a window usually of stone or concrete.

LOOK UP! GLOSSARY of STYLES

CLASSICAL GREEK ARCHITECTURE
The architecture of ancient Greece from approximately 900 BC to 1 AD. It is best known for temples with formal plans and decoration. The Greek style of Architecture emphasizes symmetry, balance, and proportion.

CLASSICAL ROMAN ARCHITECTURE
Roman Architecture spans the period from approximately 500 BC to the 4th century AD. The Roman style is known for many advanced building types including aqueducts, arenas, theatres, and basilicas. Arches, vaults and domes are common elements of Roman Architecture.

ROMANESQUE ARCHITECTURE
A medieval architectural style used from the 6th century to the 10th century. The Romanesque style is known for massive walls, arches, vaults, and towers. Many of the buildings are modeled after medieval castles.

GOTHIC ARCHITECTURE
Gothic Architecture spans the 12th to the 16th centuries. The Gothic style is most remembered for the many great churches and cathedrals built throughout Europe during this period. The style is characterized by the pointed arch, soaring buttresses, large windows and spires.

RENAISSANCE ARCHITECTURE
Renaissance Architecture was built in Europe for over 200 years from the 1400s through the 1600s. The Renaissance combined the classical Greek and Roman styles adding more complicated proportions, symmetries, and geometric shapes. The style is considered the rebirth of the classics.

BAROQUE ARCHITECTURE
Baroque Architecture was first seen in the late 1500s. The Baroque style resembles the Renaissance style but is more flashy and expressive. It is known for being very dramatic. There are intense contrasts of light and shadow and big embellishments.

NEOCLASSICAL ARCHITECTURE
Neoclassical Architecture began in the middle of the 1700s. It brought us back to the old Roman and Greek classical styles. The "new classical" emphasized the purity of the original architecture of Europe and an effort to recreate that.

FRENCH SECOND EMPIRE ARCHITECTURE
The style of architecture used during the reign of Napolean III of France when he rebuilt Paris in the mid 1800s. The most consistent feature is the "mansard roof." Ornate doors, windows and decorative brackets were also popular. Often associated with the VICTORIAN STYLE in the United States.

BEAUX ARTS ARCHITECTURE
Beaux Arts architecture was another style brought from France. It was fashionable in the United States in the early 1900s. Beaux Arts uses Classical Architecture and adds lots of elaborate decoration and sometimes oversized features.

ART DECO ARCHITECTURE
Popular in the United States between 1920 and 1940, Art Deco combines the simple, romantic, folk forms and craft motifs with industrial materials. Typical examples include bold geometric shapes and large ornamentation.

MODERN ARCHITECTURE
The modern architectural style was introduced in the early 20th century. It was inspired by new technology and engineering developments worldwide. New building materials became available like iron, steel, and sheet glass. Larger and higher buildings were created with big windows and less structure. The buildings were stripped of decoration and modeled after the idea that "form follows function."

POST MODERN ARCHITECTURE
Post Modern Architecture emerged in the late 1970s. Post Modern characteristics are whimsical and fun unlike the simplicity of the modern style. Post Modernism mixes many different styles and adds back ornamental details. The ornament is a modern exaggeration of previous classical styles.

This book would never have been imaginable without the encouragement and support of my husband, David.

I would also like to thank my team at Lauren Rubin Architecture for their motivation and creativity.

Laura Knight Keating, for her words and dedication.

Audrey Choi, Katarzyna Kuta and Rebecca Kent for their talent and commitment.

Amelia Modlin for putting the final spark into Look Up! New York.